# THE ART OF DRESSAGE

Also by *Alois Podhajsky*

MY DANCING WHITE HORSES
THE WHITE STALLIONS OF VIENNA
THE COMPLETE TRAINING OF HORSE AND RIDER
THE LIPIZZANERS
MY HORSES, MY TEACHERS
THE RIDING TEACHER

# THE ART OF DRESSAGE

*Basic Principles of Riding and Judging*

## Alois Podhajsky

TRANSLATED BY

Eva Podhajsky

*With 28 photographs of the medalists at
the Olympic Games dressage tests 1912 to 1972
by Werner Menzendorf and others*

DOUBLEDAY & COMPANY, INC.
GARDEN CITY, NEW YORK
1976

The photographs of the medalists of the Olympic Games dressage tests 1912–1972 were made by Werner Menzendorf with the exception of photographs Nos. 2 and 5 (Photo Eilert), and No. 9 (Gene Willson Ross). Photographs Nos. 3, 7, 8, and 10, for which the photographers are unknown, were provided by the Swedish embassy in Vienna. We regret having been unable to procure a photograph of Captain Blixen-Finecke, bronze medalist in 1912.

The English language version of the Grand Prix de Dressage tests from the 1972 Olympic Games appears here by the kind permission of the Fédération Equestre Internationale, Avenue Hamoir, 1180 Bruxelles.

*The Art of Dressage* was published originally under the title *Reiten und Richten*—Erfahrungen und Vorschläge, by Nymphenburger Verlagshandlung GmbH, München.

Copyright © by Nymphenburger Verlagshandlung GmbH, München, 1974 English translation copyright © 1976 by Doubleday & Company, Inc., Garden City, New York.

Library of Congress Cataloging in Publication Data

Podhajsky, Alois.
    The art of dressage.

    Translation of Reiten und Richten.
      1. Dressage. 2. Dressage—Judging. 3. Dressage tests. 4. Grand Prix de Dressage. I. Title.
SF309.5.P62413      798'.23
ISBN 0-385-01552-6
Library of Congress Catalog Card Number 75–21241

# Contents

| | | |
|---|---|---|
| | Introduction | 1 |
| 1 | The Rider | 5 |
| 2 | The Judge | 9 |
| 3 | The Art of Riding | 15 |
| 4 | Various Dressage Tests and Their Requirements | 26 |
| 5 | Systems of Judging | 55 |
| 6 | The Grand Prix de Dressage and Judging at the Olympic Games 1912 to 1968 | 70 |
| 7 | Grand Prix de Dressage in Munich, 1972 | 97 |
| 8 | Criteria of Classical Riding | 165 |
| | In Memoriam, Alois Podhajsky by Berthold Spangenberg | 178 |
| | Index | 181 |

# Introduction

The participation in dressage classes and the judging of dressage tests in a horse show are two closely related activities. Practised seriously, both serve to maintain and improve the standard of riding in our time. The correlation of rider and judge should open new paths to mutual understanding and should provide to both inspiration and stimulus for their work. Always, the endeavours of rider and judge must be governed by the attempt to reach the goal of classical riding, namely, the education and submission of the horse in accordance with a tradition that goes back to antiquity.

Numerous books about the classical art of riding have laid down its principles. They give evidence of the degree of knowledge and the standard of riding attained in their time. Moreover, in earler years, the regulations for mounted troops in the various countries were based upon these books. In the nineteenth and the beginning of the twentieth centuries particularly, these instructions decisively influenced the development of the modern sport of riding. In many countries, during the last hundred years, equestrian associations were formed, which in most cases were the organizers of horse shows and competitions.

These associations are subordinate to their national federation, which in the United States is the American Horse Shows Association (AHSA). The national federation publishes its own rule book setting forth regulations for the training of the horse in general and for the participation in equestrian events in the particular country.

In 1921 the Fédération Equestre Internationale (FEI) was founded for the purpose of promoting the sport of riding. Its role is that of a holding company which influences and directs every field of equestrian sport and makes the final decisions.

The regulations set forth in the rule books must be respected equally by rider and judge. They point to the one aim of classical riding, which is fixed for the performer as well as for the judge. In show jumping penalty points are scored for faults or excess of time, a procedure which may be observed and checked by any attentive onlooker with some understanding of the rules. This method of scoring is a good deal simpler than that used for dressage classes and guarantees a much smoother show operation.

Dressage classes, on the contrary, all too often convey the impression that rider and judge consider each other antagonists, which seems especially apparent in the case of the rider who did not win the test. Such cases are not, unfortunately, rare incidents but to an alarming degree have become the rule at shows. They stand in flagrant contradiction to the aims of the "classical art of riding" or the "chivalrous sport," as it is so often proclaimed. There are a number of reasons for these unpleasant phenomena: lack of self-control on the part of the rider and his trainer to begin with; inability to assess one's own performance and that of the other competitors; even an insufficient command of the vast subject matter which is crowded into the general concept of "equestrian training."

Every rider should enlarge his knowledge by studying books on the subject and the rules issued by the federations. Every judge *must* have a profound knowledge of the official rules, for they alone qualify him to pass a valid judgement. This requirement, together with a gift for observation and quick thinking, is generally adequate for jumping competitions.

The requirements for dressage competitions, however, are of a different sort. Here an intense study of the subject is expected from the rider and even more so from the judge. The knowledge of the official regulations is to be completed and sustained by thorough study of literature on the art of riding in general and on dressage riding in particular. And above all, there must be personal experience in the saddle.

The scoring of dressage competitions is often of greater consequence than is generally assumed, which demonstrates the importance of the comments above. In this respect large international competitions exert a greater influence on the sport of riding in general than do less important shows, since for the former noted experts are invited to judge or evaluate the scoring of the tests. A detailed study of the dressage tests of the Olympic Games since 1912 affords the best means of evaluating the actual standard of dressage presented in the Grand Prix de Dressage at the twentieth Olympic Games held in Munich in 1972. There, during the presentations of the individual test as well as the ride-off, I recorded my observations on tape. My evaluations are based on the regulations of the Fédération Equestre Internationale. The conclusions drawn from these evaluations—in comparison with the official scorings, especially—have strengthened my decision to complete this book, a project that had been planned for some time. And it is apparent that in this study there is occasion to raise a warning finger against any deviation from the tradition that established the means of co-operation for generations of horses and riders.

# 1
# The Rider

Riding is a wholesome sport which improves the physical abilities of horse and rider, balance and suppleness in particular, and which is of outstanding pedagogical value for the human partner. This educational influence, especially on self-control and self-criticism as well as courage and quick reaction, sets the sport of riding apart from other athletic activities. In recent years its importance for physical development has been underlined by the success of riding centers for the handicapped established in some countries.

As with any other sport so with riding, certain physical and mental requirements have to be fulfilled at the outset. With riding the psychological aspects are of special consequence for a good reason. The "instrument" of the sport is a living creature, that is, an individual with weak and strong points just as may be found in human beings. Therefore, respect for the living creature must be present in any person determined to practise the sport of riding in any form. This attitude will make his four-legged partner a willing friend. The horse should not be a tool which affords an opportunity to rule the world "on one's high horse" and to collect honours and ribbons in horse shows.

Right from the start the rider should set a goal for his endeavours and strive towards it with method and system. It would take us too far from the purpose of this work to go into detail here, but particulars may be found in my *Complete Training of Horse and Rider* and *The Riding Teacher* as well as in other books about jumping and dressage. Let us just draw the picture of a rider far enough advanced in his training to be allowed to think of participating in a show. Before entering in a dressage class the rider should be well aware of the general requirements made upon a participant in a horse show. He must be capable of assessing whether he has, in fact, reached the necessary standard of training. The ability to judge himself clearly will depend on his having not only the necessary practical experience but also the indispensable theoretical knowledge. Theory is the knowledge, practice the ability. One is not complete without the other, but knowledge must always take precedence over action.

At the beginning of the logical development of training the rider becomes acquainted with his horse and learns to understand him. The first goal will be reached when the physical and mental balance of horse and rider is established. Since our four-legged partner does not have the gift of language, the trainer should particularly concentrate on observation of the horse and of his reactions in all phases of the daily work. This will enable him to draw conclusions, even from insignificant signs, regarding his temperament, intelligence, and character, and will teach him to understand his partner. It is the only true way to lay the foundation of confidence and mutual understanding which at later periods produce performances of the highest standard and with full harmony between horse and rider. Mental balance of a horse must come along with physical balance.

In the formation of the rider, balance plays the same important role. He must learn to adapt the weight of his body to the rhythmic movements of the horse without disturbing him. Consequently the first thing to practise is the independent seat in the saddle as the means to convey his aids to the horse in the correct and, most important, consistent manner. To that end he needs help from a person who controls and corrects his form in the saddle. And here we come to the third partner, the trainer or riding teacher or, sometimes, just another helpful rider. His task is to observe, correct, and give advice, provided he possesses the requisite knowledge stemming from personal practical experience. I have discussed the details of the partnership of horse, rider, and instructor in my book *The Riding Teacher*.

Participation in dressage competitions offers an opportunity for the rider to assess the degree of training he and his horse have reached and to compare with other horses and riders. For this reason it is warmly to be welcomed. However, on no account must the striving for trophies and ribbons outweigh the original object of a competition, namely, to gain ideas and guidelines for further work. For in a dressage test all three, horse, rider, and trainer, submit themselves to the evaluation of the judge. Rider and teacher should draw the right conclusions from the well-founded critique of the judge, and set up a further program of work accordingly. By no means must the blame be laid on the horse when his movements or behaviour betray faults which the rider and teacher perpetrated long ago during the preparatory work. As stated above, the great educational value of the sport of riding is to be sought in the development of self-control and self-criticism.

This chapter should not be brought to an end without stating explicitly that in his striving for success the rider must never sacrifice conscientious progressive training to superficial work hastened by short cuts. The resulting nervousness and hectic atmosphere produce physical and mental tensions which entail all sorts of set-backs and bring us farther away from our goal. In vivid contrast stand the results reaped by patience. Patience alone guarantees well-founded and lasting success. The requisite time, as a rule, depends on the conformation, the intelligence, and the character of the horse and, of course, on the knowledge of the rider. Therefore, it is of varying duration.

The rider should never miss an opportunity to enlarge his knowledge and experience. For the sport of riding makes us constantly aware of the fact that even after years of activity we have not reached the end of learning.

# 2
# The Judge

The duties of a dressage judge have been briefly outlined in the preceding chapter. It is his task to evaluate and score the performance presented in a test. By giving expert reasons for his critique he points to shortcomings in training and gives the rider a guideline for correcting these faults. This obligation makes great demands on the knowledge as well as on the character of a judge. In a dressage competition he stands as much in the public spotlight as the rider. The rider is expected to make an impeccable appearance before the jury and concentrate fully on his test. Similarly, the judge should direct his undiverted attention to horse and rider from the moment they enter the dressage arena. He follows every phase of the test, taking it in chronologically as with a film camera, and setting down his observations and remarks in the records.

It is important that he forget anything that he may know about the reputation of horse and rider. He must put out of his mind whether he likes or dislikes the rider, how he performed when he saw him last, or what he may have heard about him and his horse in any previous show. In a jumping competition it is of no interest whether the rider succeeded in making a clear round in last week's competition. It is the result of the day that counts. It is exactly the same with a dressage class. The judge evaluates only what is presented in the test before his eyes and gives his reasons in the minutes. In doing so he should bear in mind that not only his verdict but also his personal attitude at the judge's table are under minute and often critical observation by the public. A dressage competition is no private club for the exchange of social or hippological gossip. It is no occasion to tell funny stories, even the best ones.

Judging is a moral obligation and must be considered as such in every respect if the judge's authority is to be preserved.

In most other sports the judges are chosen for their personality, for having practised the sport themselves, or for still practising it. This is especially true for those sports in which the performances cannot be measured by technical instruments. This principle applies to an even greater extent to the judging of dressage classes. Admittedly, even without having been an active rider, a judge can have studied from books and learned theoretically how certain exercises should be performed. In the development of the form of horse and rider the goal is an image of perfection which, as yet, is hardly ever obtained. In performing a test the rider may come nearer to this ideal at times and at others deviate from it. If he comes close to the image of perfection he should be scored higher. His marks must be lower when he remains remote from the ideal. Consequently, the faculty to decide these nuances can be presumed only in the judge who as a rider has experienced personally during the training of his own horse at what moment and in which manner this aim may be approached. Here it should once more be underlined that the judge himself must be or have been a rider.

For the sake of fairness it should be admitted that even an outstanding rider cannot by his achievements alone be proved qualified as a judge. For it is possible that a rider with talent and sensibility achieves the schooling of his horse and produces good performances without, however, being able to explain how he obtained these results. Such a rider is neither a good teacher nor a good judge. Of course, he would be better qualified to judge in any case than a person who has never himself performed in the saddle what he is called upon to judge in others.

It is largely due to the appointment of such unqualified persons that the authority of the judge has seriously diminished and is often questioned. This fact becomes more and more obvious and is one of the reasons for many an unpleasant incident, as mentioned earlier, so detrimental to competitive sport. Riders are not willing to acknowledge the mere authority of office but would bow to the authority of competence based on knowledge and achievements. The anti-authoritarian attitudes of our time cannot alter the fact that the sport of riding is not itself improved by such notions even if they are called "modern concepts." The proof is in the lower and lower standards to be observed in dressage riding in general.

While in former years the cavalry schools controlled and maintained the equestrian standards in most countries, this duty now falls mainly upon the judge. Therefore, apart from his keen gift of observation and the integrity of his character, the judge *must* possess profound knowledge of riding. The judge must have a precise concept of the training of a dressage horse to be able to detect faults immediately, determine their cause, and take them into account when scoring. It should be noted, though, that often a very obvious fault is caused by the present situation and is of much less importance than another which springs from shortcomings in basic training and is therefore to be penalized much more severely even if it is perhaps not as clearly detectable. At the risk of being accused of repetition, I want to stress once more that such discernment is possible only from a judge with personal experience in training horses.

Here let us enumerate what should be expected and required in a dressage class according to the principles of classical riding:

1. A straight horse going forward with impulsion.
2. Absolute purity of the paces and regularity of the steps. These convey beauty to the riding horse and may truly be called the music of movement.
3. The horse should accept the bit with calmness and confidence and submit willingly and spontaneously to the guidance of his rider. It is the horse that should seek this guidance. On no account should the rider force the horse into a determined position of head and neck by means of the reins. Collection obtained in this incorrect manner is invariably betrayed by the lack of freedom of the paces.
4. Suppleness of the horse must have been obtained and improved by logically built-up gymnastic training. It is reflected in the smoothness of the movements, in fluent transitions, and, last but not least, in the absolute balance in all exercises. This balance can be obtained only when sufficient energy is present in the hind quarters

of the horse, which take their full or greater share in carrying the rider's weight. When the horse moves in this manner, he conveys the impression that, in terms of mechanics, the motor as the source of movement is located in the hind quarters and its driving power is guided and regulated by the reins in the rider's hands.

5. The horse's physical proficiency is mainly the result of his suppleness provided there are absolute physical self-control and perfect balance. It is manifested in the correctness of the exercises with regards to the sequence of the steps as well as the preciseness of figures. This adroitness should become obvious in any phase of the test, not only in the difficult movements of the more advanced classes but also in the collected paces and in the performance of simple exercises such as voltes and halts.

6. The horse's obedience, the most important requirement of a dressage horse, is mentioned last for a good reason. Obedience is the logical result of the above-mentioned requirements having been fulfilled. It must never be that of a drilled poodle. It should be the proud achievement of gymnastic training of the horse based on preservation of his willingness and individuality.

These principles of classical riding should and must be observed as the main elements in the performance of a dressage horse. This is to be very clear to every rider and even more so to every judge. For the clarity of concepts is of utmost importance for any kind of co-operation. The performance and training of the horse should be without mystery, and the announced decision of the judge should be without occultism. The reasons which as a rule have to be given for any verdict should not be drowned in a flow of technical terms and sophisticated words but must be simple and clear so as to be understood by any rider and even by an attentive observer. The judge with a sense of duty and responsibility should conscientiously fulfill this demand in the interest of a branch of the sport of riding which rightfully calls itself classical. The improvement of understanding between rider and judge is of utmost importance if dressage riding is to continue to be practised in the future and find sufficient friends and followers. At that point the judge will no longer have to fear for his authority.

# 3
# The Art of Riding

The art of riding may be traced back through several thousands of years. In some periods of history riding developed into art and in others it sank to a low level and was practised by rule of thumb.

The coexistence of horse and man may be ascertained in prehistoric times, for in archaeological sites the bones of man have been found next to skeletons of horses. These excavations prove that the horse was appreciated above the other domestic animals and was buried at the side of his master. As yet, we do not know in what way the horse rendered his first service to man, whether it was in harness or under saddle or as a pack-horse. But in view of archaeological findings we may presume that the domesticated horse was first used for riding. Earthen plates found on the site of the former capital of the Hittites and dated over three thousand years old contain "directions for the breeding and the training of horses." These minute and even pedantic regulations suggest that the origin of riding is to be sought in even darker depths of history in East Asia and as early as two thousand years before Christ.

The importance accorded to the horse as a mount by the Assyrians is revealed to us in stone bas-reliefs dating from approximately 1600 B.C. They suggested a highly de-

veloped standard of riding. The unknown artist must
have had models of flesh and blood, riders firm in the saddle as they hunted lion or shot their arrows from the
backs of galloping horses.

The frieze of the Parthenon and especially Xenophon's
book, which dates from the fourth century B.C., give evidence of the high standard of riding in those days. Rightfully they are called the oldest documents of the classical
art of riding. And the fact that a statesman, general, phi-
losopher, and pupil of the great Socrates so engrossed
himself in the art of riding underlines its importance.
Xenophon was one of the first, if not the first, to see the
psychological aspects of equitation, which increase the
understanding of riding in general. Moreover, the equestrian art, more than any other, is intimately linked to the
wisdoms of life. Indeed, many of its principles may serve
as guidelines for human behaviour, and through the centuries this knowledge has been applied as a valuable
means of education.

The following sentence from Xenophon's book should
be repeatedly emphasized: "The art of riding is based on
rewards and punishments." This principle was unfortunately not always observed by later followers of the noble
art. Today's riders should memorize and take to heart
Xenophon's further instructions: "Never should you treat
your horse in anger, for there is something blind in anger
which makes us commit actions that later will be regret-
ted." And then there is the wonderful insight: "Anything
forced or misunderstood can never be beautiful. If a
dancer were forced to dance by whips and spikes, he
would be no more beautiful than a horse trained under
similar conditions."

Any sport, any art, any culture are subject to Nature's

law of rise and decline. Often after a fall there is no rise for a long time. This was the case with the art of riding after the decline of Greek hegemony, and, later, the detrimental effects of the mass migrations. The art of riding gradually deteriorated and finally even lost the semblance of true art. In the sixteenth century, along with the renaissance of fine arts, the long forgotten art of riding was revived at last, and through the centuries was fervently advocated and spread by such great riding masters as Pluvinel, Guérinière, Weyrother, Oeynhausen, Steinbrecht, Heydebreck, and Stensbeck, to name a few of the most outstanding.

The principles of classical riding are here summarized briefly and without details. The emphasis is on those concepts which are important for both rider and judge in today's dressage classes. The classical art of riding is based upon a thorough study of the horse's talents and abilities and of the means of communication with him. Through the centuries a comprehensive literature has been compiled on the subject. And yet, classical riding is nothing else but the cultivation of the movements of the horse as shown when at liberty as well as of those which are developed when the horse is ridden. Consequently, the schooling of a horse according to the classical concept should be built up as follows:

1. Riding the horse in a natural position of head and neck in the ordinary paces and on straight lines—that is, riding freely straight forward. This kind of riding may be an end in itself.

2. Riding the collected horse in all paces and turns in perfect balance. This phase of riding is possible only on the foundation of the previously practised first phase and represents its only possible development.

3. Riding the horse with greater collection and with an increased position of head and neck together with an intensified flexion of the three joints of the hind legs. Regularity, suppleness, and proficiency are now demanded in all ordinary paces as well as in less ordinary ones that may be copied from nature. This degree of perfection obtained by methodical training is called "High School" or "Haute Ecole." This third phase of riding is unthinkable without the two previously mentioned. The High School is to be considered as a whole, uniting all three phases of riding—so much so that the correctly schooled dressage horse may be taken out on a cross-country course and over simple obstacles at any given moment.

When one thinks seriously about the meaning of these three phases of training, it will become obvious how preposterous are the notions of a "modern" concept of dressage which one hears nowadays. And, in fact, the demands made upon a well-trained dressage horse, as laid down in the concise rules of the FEI, are identical with the classical principles.

Here and now a few words should be said about the individual "Germanic" or "Romanic" styles of riding frequently discussed but never fully explained. On principle and in the interest of the international sport of riding, such classification is to be rejected. As clearly seen in the historical development of the art of riding, there is no such thing as "Germanic" or "Romanic" riding or art of riding. Stimulated by the renaissance of this art in Europe in the sixteenth century, riding academies were founded in various countries and studies were made at the famous riding academies and with the famous riding masters of the time in Italy and France in order to improve and perfect the standard. Consequently, all instruction was drawn from the same source. It was not until the end of the last century that one or another rider has tried to explain away his personal weaknesses by saying that this was his nation's concept of riding. Certainly, nations prominent in the sport of riding have occasionally produced riding masters with revolutionary ideas. But in most cases such charlatans have been properly taken care of on their home grounds.

Man is fallible and a method of training, even the best, is impaired by wavering or mediocre representatives. But this should not lead to sticking a new label on a method of training debased by human weakness and praising it as the only true method. It seems to be presumptious to try to replace the teachings of a Guérinière or one of the other great old masters by new, so-called "modern" methods. At the very best the result would be, as can unfortunately be seen too often, that the rider may make work easier for himself. However, he loses in double and treble measure what according to Xenophon and Guérinière he should strive for, namely, the horse that develops to his full beauty, that submits to man willingly and with joy, and that by his suppleness and proficiency makes riding a sheer pleasure.

"Modern" interpretation is a term used mainly to cover up superficial and fast work and can only lead to the decline of the art of riding which for centuries has brought beauty and harmony to mankind. The bill is already presented in the unfortunate low standard of riding in our time. How very sad it is for today's breeders, for never before have riders had the choice of such beautiful horses.

We should not close our eyes to the fact that the art of riding has undergone various periods of crisis. This is in accordance with a law of nature that we cannot deny. But we must try to learn from these periods of decline. We must not simply shrug them off as unavoidable or, worse, try to explain them away with fake technical terms invented expressly for the occasion.

In this connection I want to quote a few interesting lines from the book *The Noble Horse,* written by the German Baron G. Biel and published in Dresden in 1830. The author begins a chapter with the statement that a sad state of affairs prevailed in most German riding schools, that the horses were overbent, their heads pulled down in an unnatural manner, and that one sought in vain for examples of the true art of riding. He continues literally: "I came to Vienna and watched the riders of the Spanish Riding School. I felt that riding was practised on different principles than in those riding academies I had visited previously. By conversing with the riding master Max Ritter von Weyrother my ideas about the art of riding became clarified. The equestrian art is a valuable, most important ally of the breeder. I would consider myself very lucky if I could breed horses for an institute following the principles of the Spanish Riding School. Nobody would then dare to maintain that the noble English horse was not suitable for the art of riding."

Riding master Weyrother was the most outstanding representative of classical riding of his time. His influence was beneficial for military equitation as well as for the sport of riding in all Europe, for the principles of the classical art of riding set the guidelines for dressage riding in general.

To what extent these guidelines apply to the different methods of judging and must be considered in scoring is summarized in the following pages. Utmost attention must be directed to the purity of the paces and the regularity of the steps of a dressage horse. In the most difficult classes and after having been trained in the High School movements such as piaffe and passage, the dressage horse should have preserved his natural paces. Indeed, physically and mentally developed by intelligent training, he should present them with even greater beauty and brilliance. One of the great riding masters was correct in saying that nature can exist without art but not art without nature. Consequently, the well-trained dressage horse should perform the natural paces with perfection. Any defects in these movements cannot be made up for by some other spectacular exercises. Riders or judges who allow themselves to be dazzled by such striking movements betray the true art of riding.

Therefore, it must be expected from a dressage horse, whether in a simple preliminary test or in the Olympic Grand Prix, that he show a pure walk gaining ground to the front, and an elastic, regular, and impulsive trot. The canter should consist of lively and rhythmic bounds in any of the three speeds and must not in collection degenerate to a limp of four beats.

These generally valid demands made upon a dressage horse provide the infallible criteria for the judge when assessing the correctness of training. Faults that appear here are fundamental and should not be minimized. It is frequently said that dressage is not an end in itself but a means to obtain a purpose. If this be so, the dressage horse has to maintain his natural free paces which must not be sacrificed to any so-called High School exercises. What is expected from a dressage horse trained in the principles of classical riding? Above all that he is smooth in his movements and comfortable for his rider! This can never be true of a horse that moves with irregular and tense steps. Besides, not being supple and proficient, he falls short of the rest of the demands and will also be worn out prematurely. For a horse is supple and agile only when in a state of complete relaxation—the very opposite of tension.

The extent to which the confusion of concepts about the training of dressage horses has grown is demonstrated by the remark of a well-known dressage rider. He wondered why he should supple up and relax his horse before the test when later on he would need him tense for the passage. This fundamental confusion must be nipped now. There should be impulsive movements, yet the horse should be supple and relaxed; the rider should maintain a straight position and at the same time be supple and smooth; these and many other aspects appear to be contradictory but raise riding from the level of craftmanship to that of art.

As said before, the first and most important demand for all classes of dressage tests remains the purity of the paces and an obedient, supple, and dexterous horse. Suppleness and dexterity are the result of systematic gymnastic training. Some horses by nature have enough suppleness but lose it temporarily when at the beginning of schooling they are hampered by the rider's weight. Others possess this natural suppleness to a lesser degree. With these horses sufficient flexibility has to be produced gradually by methodical training. It is well known that with human beings, too, many a physical weakness may be eliminated by systematic gymnastics. Suppleness, proficiency, and fitness of the horse complement each other and to the attentive observer are most obviously reflected in his smooth movements. In most cases the rider's position reveals the degree of the horse's suppleness. For a horse that makes his rider bounce up and down in the saddle at the trot is not sufficiently supple. This bouncing up and down points to a stiff back or to stiff joints of both fore- and hind legs and becomes noticeable also in the horse's tense steps.

I have discussed the importance of regular and supple movements at such length in this chapter because on one hand they are fundamental for the rider's steady and smooth seat from which he derives the ability to give the aids in a constant and consistent manner. On the other hand they give the judge infallible proof of the correct training and honest presentation of the horse.

The horse's suppleness as well as the lightness with which he accepts the actions of the reins are best judged in the changes of tempo, which should not only be clearly noticeable but also smooth and fluent. Considering dispassionately the present state of affairs in dressage tests, we must say we miss the performance of clear changes of tempo in even the advanced classes. In most cases the riders settle for some unvarying medium speed which in the extension is increased to a few tense strides after which the rider apparently thinks he has presented an effective program.

But what does the classical school prescribe in this respect? The horse should maintain an even rhythm of movement and just lengthen or shorten the stride according to the speed demanded. Transitions performed in this manner alone convey the impression of beauty. At the same time they prove that the horse is supple and smooth in his movements and in perfect balance. Should this not be expected from any dressage horse?

Even in the Olympic dressage tests of the past decades

experts stated that few horses showed a true collected trot. Most horses slowed down the sequence of steps and often produced more or less hovering steps somewhere between trot and passage. But the degree of difficulty of this test is just that. A horse having mastered piaffe and passage should be able to perform a rhythmic and lively collected trot as evidence of the correct balance and suppleness which are the basis of his physical proficiency.

In the dressage tests of recent years it has become obvious to the expert how difficult the simplest exercises—such as correctly going through a corner or the precise performance of a volte—are for some horses. How negligibly small is the number of riders able to execute the correct figure of eight or double voltes at the trot or canter! The two voltes are rarely ever of the same size because hardly a horse is evenly flexed and supple on both sides and consequently stiffens against the inside rein.

Furthermore, obedience is demanded from a dressage horse. It is the most noticeable characteristic but often tempts the judge to overlook any shortcomings in the previously mentioned requirements. Misjudgement is often due to this overlooking. For it is not just the horse's obedience that is decisive but the *manner* in which he follows his rider's commands. Were it for obedience alone, all those riders would triumph who by all sorts of forcible means bring their horses to execute their orders mechanically. Typical examples occur in the piaffe required in the Olympic dressage test. The majority of the horses more or less doggedly move about on the spot but very rarely do we see regular and elevated steps. This is because most horses are taught the piaffe by whip aids or by touching the hind legs with the whip. But as soon as the man with the whip is no longer there the piaffe is not either. Experience of classical riding has taught us that a horse is able to perform a correct piaffe only when he is sufficiently balanced. This balance will have been manifest in the ability to reduce the tempo correctly at the trot.

Advice given in such conciseness can, of course, only stimulate rider and judge to penetrate further into the true meaning of the equestrian art and help prevent their losing themselves in a wrong direction. The study of the literature on dressage riding in particular—once more I refer to my *Complete Training of Horse and Rider*—is explicitly recommended. A clear agreement on concepts must be established between rider and judge to give fresh impetus to dressage riding so that it may rise from the present low standard and again become an art.

This is in the interest of the sport of riding and even more of the creature entrusted to our care. The horse is exposed to all sorts of devices which are often thoughtlessly applied. He suffers from ignorance and lack of understanding and, last but not least, from rushed work. This sad mark of time is drastically underlined by the short life-span of many riding horses. The high standard of a sport does not depend on the number but on the quality of the people who practise it. Strangely enough, there has never been so much talk about the "classical art of riding" than there is today when we are so far away from the ideal. Any art, any sport must manifest itself not in words but in achievements. Nobody should speak of a dressage test at the first level of training as "classical" riding. And yet this has happened frequently in bombastic reports of horse shows. The art of riding does not, in fact, begin before the dressage tests of the Fifth Level and attains its highest aim in Haute Ecole.

# 4

# Various Dressage Tests and Their Requirements

According to the present situation the dressage classes, as a rule, are classified as follows:

1. Dressage tests for riding horses
2. Dressage tests for Three-Day-Event horses

The dressage tests for riding horses portray the progressive training of the horse and are generally divided into five classes. Deviations may be due to local conditions or the different development of the sport in different countries.

First Level – beginner's class
Second Level – simple requirements
Third Level – higher demands than at Second Level but simpler ones than in Fourth Level
Fourth Level – medium class
Fifth Level – difficult class

Dressage tests from First through Third Levels are reserved for a country's own riders, that is, they are national competitions, while the Fourth and Fifth Levels may involve international competition. Apart from these five classes of dressage tests for riding horses there is a combined dressage test called the free-style test consisting of a compulsory test and a "Kür," in which each competitor presents a program of his devising which, however, must contain a number of prescribed exercises.

In addition, three international official dressage tests have been introduced by the Fédération Equestre Internationale (FEI).

a) Prix St. George
b) Intermediate test
c) Grand Prix with a ride-off.

The Prix St. George bridges the gap between Fourth and Fifth Levels. The Intermediate test equals in difficulty the test of the Fifth Level. In the Grand Prix the degree of difficulty attains the highest level. The Grand Prix and the ride-off are required at the Olympic Games.

In a dressage test in general it is expected that the horse be straight and move forward with impulsion in all paces, that he take a calm contact with the bit and submit willingly and obediently to the guidance of his rider to whom, made supple by previous gymnastic training, he gives a pleasant ride. The horse should change paces without losing contact, allow himself to be turned and taken into the direction indicated by the rider without resistance, react to the most imperceptible aids, and perform the demanded exercises easily and without constraint. In a word, he should convey to the rider on his back the greatest happiness on this earth. As the great riding master Guérinière wrote two hundred years ago: "It is the aim of training a horse by systematic work to make him calm, supple, and obedient, pleasant in his movements, and comfortable for his rider."

By no means is the often-quoted happiness on this earth an actuality, however, as witnessed by the constant fight between horse and rider which in one form or other may often be observed on the show grounds, mostly in the warming-up area, sometimes even during the test and not in the lower classes only. The absence of this happiness is also reflected in the indifferent, even joyless faces of the dressage horses that often go mechanically through their paces with tense and irregular steps. Horse and rider in this form are not ready for participation in even the beginner's class. The judge should severely penalize such phenomena and explain his reasons in the records. His decision must never be dictated by complaisance. If it is, he is doing a bad turn to the sport of riding and contributing to the present decline of standards. The unpleasant sight of riders fighting with their horses is rightfully criticised and should not be given the opportunity to persist by the complaisance of a judge.

On the contrary, the severe but just verdict of the judge will spur many a rider to follow the lines of true riding and build up the work with his horse in the manner repeatedly outlined in this book so that the horse grows into a joyful partner and friend. The unpleasant sight would then disappear from the show grounds, and every expert, the judges included, would be pleased and grateful. Watching a show would become sheer pleasure and the members of the SPCA would have no reason to complain.

However, if a rider takes offence and withdraws from

the sport of riding out of spite and because of a justified decision of the judges, he only proves that he has not grasped the educational meaning of equitation. The disappearance from the show grounds of a rider with such obvious lack of sportsmanship would certainly be no great loss.

In this context I want to discuss once more the goal the rider should strive for and the methods he should use. If he cannot afford to ride regularly and with qualified teachers and horses, he should ride for pleasure as much as he wants but not succumb to the ambitious notion of appearing in horse shows. If he wants to participate with honours in a show, he must take the time and submit to regular and serious training, just as it is taken for granted that he would have to do with any other sport.

A dressage test of the First Level should, above all, prove that the training of horse and rider is built on the essential, correct basis. For this reason, much greater importance should be accorded to this test than is generally assumed. This level serves basically as a test of whether the young rider is sufficiently advanced and mature for any activity on a show ground. With this class, the rider should, so to speak, obtain the license that enables him to appear in public. This practice is actually followed in some countries where equestrian organizations require the rider to pass a First Level test even before being permitted to enter a jumping class. Such a regulation is of great benefit as it doubtlessly spares the public many an unpleasant sight and the horse much discomfort and harm. From the point of view of the expert it would be welcome if some moderate schooling in dressage were expected from the jumping rider as well as from the jumping horse.

The show jumper would realize the great advantages of a trained horse, and at the same time the dressage rider would be reminded that the so-called dressage of the horse must never be an end in itself but always the means to a goal.

Moreover, starting in a dressage test of the First Level would provide opportunity to a young horse to get accustomed to unfamiliar surroundings and to concentrate on performing attentively what he has learned so far. In the performance of the simple exercises demanded in such tests the rider and his teacher can best detect any shortcomings of the four-legged partner. By such understanding they can avoid increasing their demands too soon and too rapidly. The same may apply to the young rider. Therefore, even a test of the First Level calls for a judge with experience and knowledge of method, for he can and should have a decisive influence on the further training of horse and rider.

In a dressage test of the First Level the three basic paces, walk, trot, and canter, are required; specifically, medium walk, working and medium trot, and working and medium canter. The horse, in a simple snaffle, is expected to perform these paces in a pure sequence of steps. The transitions from the movement into the standstill are restricted to a halt from the medium walk and from the working trot. Those from the standstill into movement involve a move-off into the medium walk and working trot. The transitions from one pace into another play an important part in the evaluation of the degree of training the horse has reached. In the First Level it is sufficient to show transitions from a medium walk into the working and medium trot and from these two paces into the working and medium canter, as well as from the working and medium canter into the working and medium trot. There should be no transition from the canter into the walk. The changes of tempo are limited to transitions between medium and working trot and between medium and working canter and vice versa. The working tempo is a speed between the medium trot and the collected trot as well as between the medium and the collected canter. The working tempo is the preliminary step to the collected paces.

It is of special importance that the horse move in rhythmic steps and at a regular tempo around the entire arena and when changing through the arena over the diagonal. The latter exercise particularly offers an opportunity for the judge to determine whether the horse is sufficiently straight and has sufficient impulsion in order to trace the diagonal precisely and without swaying. In the case of this change of rein being effected at the working canter, the horse should be taken into the working trot a few steps before reaching the opposite side. He should then strike off into the canter on the other lead. It is inadmissible to demand a simple change of lead through the walk in a test of the First Level, because it does not comply with the degree of training the horse can possibly have reached. Since the time has not yet come for a transition from the canter into the walk, there naturally cannot be a simple change of lead at the canter. This principle must be observed by the rider and judge and even more by the authors of dressage tests in order to follow the rules of classical equitation. In the execution of a change over the diagonal in the manner just described the judge will find ample opportunity to evaluate the contact with the bit, the smoothness, suppleness, balance, and obedience of the horse.

In the performance of large circles (twenty meters in diameter) at the working trot or working canter and in a change of rein when going large from a circle, the judge may note the correct lateral flexion and the degree of suppleness as well as a confirmed contact and the horse's smooth response to the rider's rein aids. Moreover, these exercises prove the horse's training to be equal on both reins. The requirements of the test may be increased by the performance of voltes, small circles of eight steps' diameter instead of the six steps ordinarily prescribed. At the present stage of training they should be executed at the walk and at the working trot.

The halt belongs to the basic training of any useful riding horse. At the First Level it is demanded from the medium walk and from the working trot. The horse should remain in unaltered contact, cease to move, and come to a standstill in the direction of the movement and on all four legs. If he throws his head up in the transition or leans onto the bit with the whole weight of his forehand, his hind legs cannot step correctly under his body. In most cases the horse will be crooked, which gives the judge proof of incorrect contact with the bit, of a lack of balance, and of the absence of smooth response to the rein aids. These facts have to be considered accordingly in the scores.

The immediate transition from the halt into the medium walk or into the working trot is to be executed in regular and even contact with the bit in order to be classified as "good" or "very good."

The rein-back counts among the basic demands made

upon a riding horse. At this level it is limited to the length of a horse; a determined number of steps should not be required. The horse should step back diagonally in a rhythmic sequence of steps and on a straight line. He must not resist the encouraging rein aids of the rider. Neither should he creep back or, worse, hurry back to evade the control of his rider. Difficulties in this exercise are due to lack of suppleness and smooth response to the rein aids. They are also to be sought in disobedience and incorrect contact with the bit.

The correct contact with the bit may best be perceived when the rider rides on a loose rein at the walk or trot and then takes up the reins again. There should not be any change in the rhythm or tempo of movement. This exercise is demanded in some tests of this level. If there is an observable difference, the contact is faulty.

Furthermore, correct contact is proved when the rider allows the horse, by slowly lengthening his neck and gently champing the bit, to gradually take the reins from his hands at the halt, the walk, and finally at the working trot. Jerking the reins from the rider's hand, on the contrary, points to the very opposite. This behaviour and especially an open mouth with the tongue pulled up or placed over the bit are cardinal faults which must not be neglected by the judge but marked accordingly low in his scores. If such faults were passed over lightly at the initial stage of training, the correctness of further schooling would be seriously jeopardized.

It goes without saying that in any dressage test the rider's seat and his attitude on horseback should enter into consideration. The correct use of the rein and leg aids, the upright position of the body without stiffness are the elements of the unity that horse and rider should form. They reveal the gymnastic training of both creatures, which is the foundation of the entire schooling process. The Austrian cavalry inspector General Höbert used to conclude from the relaxed position of the riders the correctness of training of the young horses and from their regular movements the riders' correct aids.

Riding serpentines and dividing the arena into half and enlarging it again at the medium walk and working trot are further requirements of the beginner's class which offer the judge sufficient opportunity for fair evaluation of the standard of training of horse and rider. In some tests the turn on the forehand is demanded. In my opinion, this is overestimating the importance of this exercise. The turn on the forehand has developed from the preparatory exercise "yielding to the leg" and has no place in a dressage test, not even of the First Level.

In the First through Fourth Levels the horse is required to jump at the end of the test to prove his suppleness and obedience and, above all, his usefulness as an all-purpose riding horse. He should neither rush towards the obstacle nor hesitate but take it as with a single lengthening stride of canter and maintain the regular rhythm of the canter before and after the jump. Slight shortcomings are not marked. Penalty points are given for a refusal. Horse and rider are eliminated from the test after three refusals. The rider's attitude during the jump is evaluated along with the scores for position and seat. In a test of the First Level a jump over a simple fence of about two and a half feet is required.

On principle a young horse and a young rider should begin their career in shows in a dressage test of the First

Level. The requirements of this class are best suited to prove the correctness of their training. It is hardly possible for the young rider to gain the same beneficial experience when beginning his career in a class of the Second or Third Level.

It is open to discussion, however, whether and for what reasons an experienced dressage rider should enter his young horse in a class of the First Level. In Austrian circles of dressage riding before the war it used to be an unwritten law that the instructors of the Austrian cavalry school, for instance, and the officers who had completed their training at this institute were on principle not to present their young horses in a dressage class inferior to Fourth Level. This tacit agreement had sprung from sporting fairness and chivalrous thinking. Certain resulting advantages and disadvantages give food for thought. This arrangement was of positive value for the young riders who in the tests of the lower classes were not overshadowed by already well-known, successful horsemen who, with their experience and knowledge, were able to train and present their horses with infinitely greater skill. It was a disadvantage, though, to the experienced riders who never had an opportunity to register step by step the progress of their young horses, to gain experience with their four-legged partners and put it to practice in further training. It remains to be seen which system is of greater value for the general development of the sport of riding.

The dressage test of the Second Level represents an increase in the demands corresponding to the progress of the horse in his training. With this progress in mind, the rider must decide whether to present his horse in a snaffle or in a double bridle. In former times the double bridle was required in all dressage tests from Second Level on. It goes without saying that spurs are to be worn when the horse is in a double bridle. During the past decades the optional use of the snaffle in tests of the Second Level was introduced and is certainly to be welcomed. It positively supports conscientious schooling of the horse. In this respect the introduction of the curb represents the touchstone proving that the horse has first mastered the correct performance of all movements, turns, various speeds, transitions, and halts in the much milder snaffle.

Therefore, the requirements of the Second Level are basically the same as in the beginner's class. The demands, however, are increased by the degree of precision called for and by a number of additional exercises explained as follows.

In a dressage test the walk is of greater importance than is often understood. It is the walk, more than any other pace, that reveals most infallibly any correct or incorrect course of training. In the Second Level ordinary walk and collected walk are demanded with special attention to steady contact with the bit and regularity of the steps which must not become slower in collection but more elevated. The ordinary walk should present an obvious gain of ground to the front without, however, any increase of speed in the sequence of steps. The word "stride" interprets most vividly what is expected from a good walk.

The demands made at the performance of the trot—the backbone of the schooling of a horse—are considerably increased. The stride of the working trot is shortened into the collected trot and that of the medium trot lengthened into the extended trot. These changes of tempo repeatedly required in a test of the Second Level give the judge a chance to observe the horse's impulsion and contact with the bit as well as his physical proficiency. The collected trot should be performed not by slower steps but by shorter ones while the rhythm of the movement remains unaltered. Not hasty steps but long regular strides characterize the extended trot, which, correctly performed, impresses even the non-professional observer. To the expert it is proof of the perfect balance of horse and rider and of the vigorous activity of the hind quarters which produce a brilliant moment of suspension.

The immediate move-off from the halt into an impulsive medium trot is just as much a proof of progress in training as the direct transition from the standstill into a rhythmic collected trot with the contact unchanged. The quality of such performance must be adequately rated in the judge's scores.

The demands made at the canter are increased by frequent changes of tempo from the working canter to the medium canter. The rider is required to enter at the working canter and halt on the center line. In addition, the collected canter is demanded as well as the strike-off from the halt and from the rein-back. Furthermore, the transition from the collected canter into the halt, the strike-off on the center line from the medium walk, and a number of other exercises may be called for. The medium canter with the reins in one hand is important for the evaluation of contact and balance. From this essential exercise the judge draws interesting conclusions as to the collaboration of horse and rider. Of equal significance are the exercises "giving the reins" and "allowing the horse to slowly take the reins from the rider's hands by lengthening his neck and champing the bit." This is what is meant by the often quoted German "*Zügel aus der Hand kauen.*" In the process of training as well as in the tests the latter exercise should first be prepared and executed at the halt and walk, later at the working trot before being demanded at the working and at last at the medium canter. This reasonable development would prevent the exercise "give the reins for one long side of the arena" from being presented as it so often is at horse shows: the rider briefly pushes his hands up the horse's neck—sometimes one hand alone—and immediately applies the reins again, often after only two or three strides of canter. The judge should qualify such performance as insufficient and mark it accordingly in his scores. Besides, it reveals the rider's inflexible and hard hands, which act like a brake on the horse's hind quarters.

The simple change of lead belongs to the advanced work at the canter required in some tests of Second Level dressage. It should be performed by a correct transition into the walk and a strike-off into the canter on the other lead after two or three regular steps of clear walk.

At this stage the counter canter is demanded, on a straight line first and later also on the large circle. The elastic regular three beats of the canter and the straightness of the horse are essential for good marks. Any crookedness, especially at the canter, points to a lack of forward urge, faults in the contact with the bit, and a deficient activity of the hind quarters which should make the judge lower his scores. The transition from the collected canter into the collected trot and vice versa is of equal importance. Without hesitation and without chang-

ing contact the horse should pass into the collected trot
smoothly and with suppleness and in the same manner
strike off into the collected canter without becoming
faster or hasty if such performance is to be marked by the
judge with "good" or "very good."

In the execution of correct voltes, a circle of six steps'
diameter is demanded in the dressage tests of the Second
Level. They should be performed at the collected trot and
collected canter while maintaining the steady rhythm of
the movement and the unaltered lateral flexion. This exercise is correctly performed when the horse is bent evenly
from the poll to the tail in accordance with the curve of
the circle. The volte is a valuable means for the judge to
evaluate the suppleness and the correct contact of the
horse. Oval or angular voltes, as unfortunately may often
be seen even in tests of the more advanced classes, reveal
stiffness, uneven contact, and lack of suppleness and dexterity. Such basic faults must not be passed over lightly
by rider and teacher and even less so by the judge.

Another important piece of information about the degree of training of horse and rider is provided by a half
volte and change, that is, a half circle and return to the
track. The half volte should begin in the same manner as
a full volte. On completion of the half circle, however, the
horse is expected to return to the track on a straight line
and at an angle of forty-five degrees, remaining straight
at the counter canter which follows and not becoming
crooked by an exaggerated position to the outside. Crookedness at the counter canter is as much a fault as the
horse not coming back to the wall on a straight line but
slipping away in a sort of half pass, as is often seen even

in dressage tests of the more advanced classes. Both faults are seldom evaluated severely enough by the judges.

Among the exercises at the walk required in the dressage tests of the Second Level is the turn on the haunches. It is correctly performed when the forehand describes a small half circle around the hind legs, which move on the spot and at the rhythm of the walk. It is a lesser fault if the hind legs move on a small half circle than if one of the hind legs remains riveted to the ground or, even worse, steps back. The judge watches out for this fault as much as for any sign of resistance which becomes noticeable in loss of contact, stiff or uneven steps, or the horse throwing up his head.

As already mentioned in the description of the beginner's class, it is the obvious duty of the judge to observe closely the rider's position. An unsteady seat points to stiffness and lack of suppleness in the horse and is to be taken into account in the scores.

The jump is over a simple obstacle of approximately three feet and is marked in the same manner as in the First Level.

The dressage test of the Third Level gradually prepares for the more difficult classes and, like the previous tests, is competed on a national scale only.

An increase of impulsion and suppleness is now expected in the performance of the exercises enumerated in the description of the Second Level tests as well as an accentuated preciseness in the execution of all lines and figures. Hereby the correct preparation of horse and rider as well as their talent are revealed. As with the following classes so the tests of the Third Level are in most cases ridden in a double bridle. The tests are made more interesting by several new exercises and by a more rapid succession of the various figures.

At this level lateral work is added to the exercises prescribed for the First and Second Levels. With shoulder-in at the collected trot on the long sides of the arena the judge has the opportunity to observe the lateral position of the horse, and in particular, whether it remains the same on both reins. He verifies whether the hind quarters maintain the same rhythm as at the collected trot, which preceded the shoulder-in, and whether the hind legs remain alongside the wall of the arena. It is also important to note whether the horse bends evenly in his whole body or merely gives his neck a position to the inside. Any hesitation or any deviation of the hind quarters from the track would lower the marks given for the exercise, for they reveal faults in the co-ordination of the rider's aids—leg, rein, and weight aids—as much as the horse's lack of suppleness, dexterity, and contact with the bit.

The second lateral exercise at the trot required at this level is the half pass to the left and to the right, in our case a half pass from the center line to one of the long sides of the arena. To obtain high marks, the trot is expected to be lively and rhythmic, the horse going absolutely straight on the center line before beginning the half pass. His legs should cross rhythmically and in the direction of the long side towards which he is headed. The horse should take a quiet contact with the bit and be positioned into the direction of the movement. His body should be parallel to the long side; however, the hind quarters must never precede, which is to be marked as a severe fault. The horse's eyes should look forward and sideways which necessitates the position of his head into the direction into which he is going.

The degree of the position of the head at the shoulder-in and at the half pass is and was subjected to slight variations with riders of different nationalities. There is no reason, however, to blow it up into a big affair and try to fabricate ideas about the Germanic or Romanic concept of riding and others of the sort. Every rider knows or should know that a horse is inclined to bend less on his stiff side and consequently adopts a lesser degree of position than on his hollow side to which he generally assumes an exaggerated position of head and neck. Therefore, the judge must determine whether the lateral flexion and the position of head and neck remain the same on both reins, which proves the correctness of training and alone counts for a fair decision by the judge.

Among the exercises required at the Third Level belongs the turn on the haunches at the walk. The degree of difficulty is increased by demanding it also from the standstill. Practical experience teaches us that the turn on the haunches is easier from the walk than from the halt. From the standstill the horse must begin the movement and at the same time begin to turn. Having completed the turn, he must come again to a standstill evenly on all four legs. Considering these requirements, if performed correctly, the turn on the haunches from the halt is to be scored higher than that from the walk.

Serpentines of four loops at the working trot through the whole length of the arena demand regular impulsion and well-established contact with the bit. The horse should execute these four loops of equal size and at an

1. Captain Count Bondé on Emperor—Gold medal 1912

2. Major Boltenstern on Neptun—Silver medal 1912

3. Captain Lundblad on Uno—Gold medal 1920

4. Lieutenant Sandström on Sabel—Silver medal 1920 and 1924

5. General Linder on Piccolomini—Gold medal 1924

6. Baron von Langen on Draufgänger—Gold medal 1928

unchanged lively tempo for which the judge must especially watch.

The transition on the center line from the medium walk into the collected canter represents another increase of the demands. In this exercise the judge can best detect the slightest deviation from the straight line or the hind quarters being thrown to the side before the strike-off—provided he never takes his eyes off the slightest movement of horse and rider, which should be his constant endeavour.

The counter canter on the circle is another important exercise in which to see whether the horse remains straight at the collected canter. The degree of difficulty may be increased by demanding a change from the first circle at the counter canter through a simple change of lead into a second at the counter canter on the other rein. This exercise may be performed correctly only after conscientious and systematic schooling and gives the judge a precise idea about the degree of training of horse and rider. Increased difficulty may be added by changing the circle with a flying change of lead.

It should be known by any rider and his trainer or teacher, as well as by any judge with the necessary practical experience, that a horse can perform accurate flying changes of lead only when he has learned to move at the collected canter with energetic and active hind quarters. The best preparation consists of correct changes of tempo at the canter. If the hind legs do not jump energetically under the horse's body, a number of faults are likely to appear in the flying change, such as a four-beat canter or a half stride of the hind legs. Besides marking them in the scores the judge should call the rider's attention to these imperfections in order to prevent the faults from becoming habits which may be difficult to eliminate.

A double serpentine at the collected canter and without changes of lead is now demanded on the long side of the arena. It should be performed in regular even bounds both at the true and at the counter canter, with the horse remaining absolutely straight and in even contact with the bit. The suppleness of his movements becomes visible in the rider's elastic seat. Further degrees of difficulty are introduced by the rein-back and the transition into the collected canter. Now it is no longer a horse's length that is expected but a determined number of steps, that is, five steps of rein-back and an immediate strike-off into the collected canter. The horse should step back rhythmically and in the diagonal sequence of steps as already prescribed. The rider counts the steps and interrupts the backward movement with the fifth step without coming to a standstill. He strikes off into the collected canter immediately and without any intermediate forward steps. Not only the rider should concentrate on the correct number of steps but also the judge, who along with observing the quality of the movement must also register the number of steps. Too many steps diminish the value of the exercise just as much as too few.

The jump required at the end of this test, as at the Second Level, is approximately three feet high.

Now horse and rider have attained a degree of training that offers opportunity to measure their performance with those of riders of foreign countries. The dressage tests of the Fourth and Fifth Levels can be competed nationally or internationally. On the international level the use of the double bridle and of spurs is obligatory. It is optional on the national level.

In the dressage tests of the First through Third Level performances were required that may be expected for all purposes from a well-trained riding horse. In the Fourth Level the degree of difficulty is considerably increased. Now, for instance, the extended walk is demanded. The horse, in a pure sequence of steps, should cover the maximum ground to the front. He should lengthen his neck slightly and remain in unchanged steady contact with the bit without getting hasty in the succession of his footfalls. He should bring his hind legs well under his body, making his hind feet overstep the hoof prints of his front feet by one to three times the width of a hoof. In the extended walk the judge rewards an increased activity of the hind quarters. The more visible the activity of the hind legs, the higher the judge's score. This exercise influences the general scores in a positive way, for in the walk the correct structure of schooling is most obviously reflected—in physical as well as in mental respects. It is important to remember that the extended walk is to be performed in contact with the bit and not on a loose rein.

Trot at the different speeds is prescribed on long lines, around the whole arena or around half of it. Here is the chance to determine the impulsion expected of any riding horse and the rhythm of the movement which is to remain unchanged through the corners of the arena. Alternate sitting and rising trot at the medium and extended speeds reveal to the judge by their degree of impulsion, of suppleness, and of the absolute harmony of horse and rider the correct basic concept of schooling.

The sound foundation of training becomes obvious in

the medium canter and in the extended canter on longer lines and through the corners, which are demanded for the first time. Riding the horse with the reins in one hand or giving the reins completely conveys interesting knowledge about the co-operation of horse and rider. In these energetic exercises the rider, along with the correct influence of his seat, legs, and reins, has every opportunity to enhance the action of his horse by cadence and brilliance.

With the perfection of the collected trot and canter, exercises such as voltes, lateral work, serpentines, flying changes of lead, and counter canter through the corners of the arena succeed with brilliance and ease. From the transitions from the collected canter into the medium trot, from the collected trot into the extended trot, from the flowing changes between paces and tempi the judge determines the suppleness and lightness of the horse. The natural ease of the performance is to him a sign of the horse's attention to the rider's aids as well as of their tactfulness.

In this test haunches-in or travers, haunches-out or renvers, as well as counter changes from the center line to the long side of the arena and back to the center line are added to the lateral work required so far. The smooth and fluent succession of different lateral exercises often following each other rapidly gives the best proof of correct gymnastic training. Besides the impulsion and regular rhythm at the canter the judge watches for the correct performance of the different exercises. There are double voltes, serpentines through the length of the arena in three to four loops with or without change of lead, simple and flying changes at the canter on the center line, as well as a half volte and change of rein at the canter. The main concern in all these exercises is a straight horse at the canter as well as at the counter canter, the precise execution of lines and figures, and the harmonious rhythm of the movement.

The difficulty of this test is further increased by demanding from the horse five seconds of immobility after a halt from the collected trot or canter. The correctness of the halt is of importance to the evaluation. In addition, this exercise scores much higher if the prescribed immobility is observed.

As in Second and Third Levels the obstacle is a jump of three feet.

The exercises enumerated for the Fourth Level provide a large range of possibilities and would permit varying routines for the numerous horse shows which very often follow each other at close intervals. Unfortunately, this possibility is very seldom put to practical use. In most cases the same few standard tests are presented. This phenomenon may also be observed in the international dressage tests of the FEI.

In this connection I want to point out that in some tests for the international dressage classes a half pirouette at the collected trot is demanded. As is well known, there is the turn on the haunches at the walk and the half pirouette at the canter. A turn on the haunches at the collected trot, at the sequence of steps of the trot, that is, is unknown to classical equitation. The confusion may have developed from the misleading use of the term half pirouette for the turn on the haunches. Although this fact has been pointed out repeatedly, the half pirouette at the collected trot continued to haunt the tests for over ten years.

It is true that in the rules for the Austrian cavalry a turn on the haunches was demanded at the walk, trot, and canter. In this case, however, the horse was taken into the walk—if not already at the walk—and the turn on the haunches was performed. After completion of the turn on the haunches the horse was taken into the same pace as before, namely into trot or canter, or he continued at the walk. Consequently, at the collected canter there both, the turn on the haunches just described and the half pirouette which is to be executed in the sequence of steps of the collected canter.

The tests of the First through Fourth Level increase their demands in the same upward curve that should be followed in the judicious and conscientious schooling of the horse in the principles of classical equitation. The coordination of the demands with the degree of training is the only foundation on which horse and rider can develop to meet even higher requirements.

In the dressage tests of the Fifth Level the exercises demanded in the Fourth Level are increased in difficulty and further perfected. They come close to the requirements of the test in the Olympic Games. The test of this class may be ridden in an arena of twenty to forty meters as well as in that of Olympic dimensions, that is, twenty to sixty meters. In this test, too, the basic demands made upon a dressage horse take up a large space. They differ from those of the Fourth Level by a more rapid succession of the exercises. The figures are often to be performed on shorter lines which requires a more precise guidance on the part of the rider and a faster reaction on the part of the horse.

At the walk all three tempi are required as before. In

addition there is the extended walk with the reins in one hand. Here it must be underlined that at this extended walk the contact with the bit must not be lost although the horse is expected to lengthen his neck. In a dressage test an extended walk presented on a loose rein would severely devaluate this exercise. From my experience I want to remind rider and judge in this context that the same differentiation between "reins in one hand" and "give the reins completely" is to be observed at the trot and canter.

Shoulder-in on the center line—either towards the judges or away from them—is added to the lateral work at the trot. The judge may determine precisely whether the horse is in fact performing the shoulder-in or whether he just throws his hind quarters out. Any swaying becomes very obvious. The shoulder-in on the center line may be qualified as "good" if the hind quarters really remain straight on the center line. In the exercise of shoulder-in left on the center line up to X in the center of the arena followed by shoulder-in right down to the end of the center line, it must be clearly visible that the horse does not sway when returning his left shoulder onto the center line, going straight for a horse's length and taking the right shoulder in from the center line. This exercise serves as the proof that the horse's forward urge remains unaltered even in difficult figures.

In addition to the double counter changes already required in the previous tests, the half pass at the collected trot and canter is demanded from one long side of the arena to the opposite one. The horse should cover the distance of over twenty meters with his spine parallel to the long side, with his head clearly positioned into the direction of the movement, and at the regular rhythm of the collected trot or canter. Preceding hind quarters are counted as a fault more severe than the horse not being quite parallel to the wall.

In the classes of the Fifth Level counter changes at the collected canter are required. In this case it is of importance that the flying change be executed on a straight line and with a clear forward movement. The horse must not throw himself with his whole body into the following half pass, a fault which is due to thoughtlessly practising this exercise too often.

In this class we find among the exercises at the collected trot two voltes of six steps' diameter following each other on the center line, to the left first and then to the right or vice versa. Each volte must be of the same size and be performed at the same regular rhythm. It must end at the precise spot on the center line where it began, thus forming a figure of eight.

In the Fifth Level short half passes on either side of the center line alternating to the left and to the right and at two meters' distance from it are demanded up to five such counter changes. They are also called zigzags. It is of importance to the evaluation that the rhythm of the collected trot remain regular, that the horse maintain the correct position of his head into the direction of the movement and his lateral position without the hind quarters leading. The transition from one rein to the other should be smooth and supple with a moment's straightness and in even rhythm in order to be classified as "good" or "very good." Points should be taken off if the horse throws his body into the direction of the new half pass.

Alternating the extended trot sitting and rising serves to assess the balance of horse and rider. Here the judge closely observes whether the rhythm and the gain of ground to the front remain unchanged. Very often in the extended sitting trot the horse gains much more ground to the front than at the rising trot.

Extensive information about the suppleness, the correct contact with the bit, delicate reaction to the rider's rein, leg, and weight aids, and undiverted attentiveness as well as complete obedience of the horse is to be gained from alternating rein-back with going forward. The exercise begins with a rein-back of three to six steps followed by an immediate transition into three to six steps forward. Without coming to a standstill the horse again reins back three to six steps and proceeds immediately at the medium or extended walk, according to the program of the test. What counts for the scores is the unchanged contact with the bit when moving forward and backward as well as in the moment of transition, the correct diagonal sequence of steps, the immediate transition into the forward movement with the same pair of legs after the last of the required steps backward, and likewise the smooth rein-back instantly after the prescribed number of steps to the front has been taken. The exercise is completed when, according to the test, the horse moves forward at the medium or extended walk. The number of steps prescribed in each test must be strictly observed. It varies from three to six steps with the intention of keeping the horse from anticipating.

In a dressage test of the Fifth Level the horse is required to strike off from the halt into the collected or medium canter in such a way that the first movement after the absolute standstill is the bound of canter and there are no intermediate steps of walk or trot.

The performance of half and full pirouettes further increases the degree of difficulty of the demands made at the canter. The judge may best observe them on the center line or on the diagonal of the arena. The horse, moving at a cadenced collected canter, performs a half or full turn around his hind legs, which are the turning point and which canter on the spot. It is considered a lesser fault when the hind quarters describe a small circle around which the forehand moves. It is to be penalized severely if the horse throws himself around, jolting, and loses the steady contact with the bit, the rhythm and the suppleness of the canter, or when he remains riveted to the ground with one or both hind legs. The evaluation should be equally negative if the canter before, during, or after the pirouette, due to the extreme collection, is executed in four beats.

The requirements of a dressage test of the Fifth Level approach those of the Olympic program with the repeated performance of the flying change of lead after a determined number of bounds of canter and with the piaffe and passage, airs of Haute Ecole.

The repeated flying changes of lead are mainly demanded on the diagonal line, on the long side of the arena, and on the center line, less frequently on the circle. In the various dressage tests of the Fifth Level generally three to five flying changes after four and three strides, five to seven changes after two strides, and five to nine changes at every stride are required. To obtain high scores, the horse should execute the flying changes in a regular elastic bound of canter at the collected tempo with his hocks well under him and in a clear three beat. Equally important are the quiet contact with the bit and the correct position of head and neck, which are proof of the systematic schooling of the horse. The rider's position should be upright and quiet without being stiff, with his hands holding the reins correctly in front of his body and the legs placed in the correct spot and, above all, immobile along the horse's sides. The rider must not hop about in the saddle or throw his lower leg backward until it is parallel to the ground. The onlooker should have the impression that he merely thinks and the horse executes his thoughts. The horse, in unchanged rhythm and on an absolutely straight line, should perform the required number of flying changes which, at the repetition, must not become shorter nor faster. They should not be spoiled by the hind quarters swinging from one side to the other or the weight being thrown on the forehand. It is not only the exact number of strides which matters but also the manner in which the exercise is performed. The prescribed line must be strictly observed, which in this test especially the judge must critically take into account.

In the test of the Fifth Level the piaffe is often demanded from the halt and with most riders is the weakest spot of the entire performance. The passage succeeds better with horses used to being ridden briskly forward. On the other hand, these horses often reveal a tendency to hovering steps at the collected trot.

Most riders practise these two airs of the Haute Ecole far too early in training and neglect the consolidating fundamental work. Consequently, the obvious question arises whether piaffe and passage should be required in a Fifth Level test at all. For even at the Olympic Games they are seldom presented to perfection. In most cases the piaffe is executed as an irregular stumbling on the spot. It might certainly contribute to a higher standard of dressage riding if the most difficult movements of classical equitation, piaffe and passage, remained reserved for the Grand Prix as the highest dressage test.

Occasionally, combined dressage tests are organized in national or international horse shows. They consist either of a standard test and stadium jumping or, more often, of a standard test chosen from the list of Fifth Level tests and a free-style "Kür" in which the rider presents a program of his own devising in a given space of time. On principle, the exercises performed in a Kür should not exceed in difficulty those prescribed for the standard test. The judge in scoring must not take into account any extra work of an over-ambitious rider trying to outdo his opponents.

The international dressage tests of the International Equestrian Federation are discussed in detail in Chapter 6, "The Grand Prix de Dressage and Judging at the Olympic Games 1912 to 1968."

The requirements of the dressage test in the Combined Training in national horse shows generally follow the demands made upon horse and rider in the dressage tests of the Second Level. In accordance with the over-all intention of this class, however, the extended canter is included in the test. The program of the dressage test of international Combined Training comes nearer to the Third Level dressage test by including certain exercises such as, for instance, half pass at the trot. However, there are well-founded doubts as to the utility of a half pass to the training of a cross-country horse.

# 5
# Systems of Judging

The modern sport of riding as seen in today's horse shows began to develop in Europe around the turn of the century. Initially, it was considered predominantly the province of the army. Often these shows were called by their French name, *concours hippique*. In these pages the systems of judging to be discussed are those related to the competitions which in old Austria were called "prize riding" and which are now known as "dressage tests." The term dressage is not too happy a one, for it suggests something like the drilling of a poodle, that is, the very opposite to what is expected from the training of a horse according to the principles of classical horsemanship. But since the term has become the international one for this kind of riding, we must accept it. After all, it is not the name that is of importance but the manner in which this sport is practised.

In Austria, prize riding and, later, dressage classes originally consisted of a preliminary and a principal test. In the preliminary test the competitors in turn rode upon command a program composed by one of the judges shortly before. A jury consisting of one to three judges evaluated the performances and decided the placements of the contestants.

In the principal test, which was ridden on the show grounds before the public, all riders had to present their horses in a group and upon command. This presentation in a group gave an opportunity to watch the behaviour of the horses under varied conditions and afforded a comparison of the performances of the different riders. At that point the final placing was determined and the result might be affected by any disturbance during the presentation or by a distinct inferiority to the performance shown in the preliminary test. This was, without a doubt, a very wise arrangement because it allowed for consideration of faults occurring during the principal test or any visible decline of the general form of a rider. The final verdict announced was understood by the general public, the majority of which had not seen the preliminary test. Thus there was a positive contact between observer and judge. It should be mentioned, however, that in the years up to the Second World War, such large groups of starters as populate today's horse shows were unknown. There were rarely more than ten to twelve competitors. A decision made after two tests at two different places is certainly more comprehensive and, above all, offers a more precise evaluation of the equestrian training of the candidates. The hazard of misjudgement was eliminated to a large extent when the judge was able to see horse and rider in the same or in similar exercises for a second time. And in performing at different places the confidence of the horse in his rider is put to the test. Confidence in his rider is a basic characteristic of a good riding horse, although it may depend to a certain degree on the temperament of the four-legged partner.

In any case, it should not be necessary for the dressage rider to have his horse examine the arena or inspect the judge's stand before the test. It has even happened that the judges were blamed for the rider's failing because of some abrupt movement or the use of a typewriter. It is sad evidence of a rider's weaknesses and shortcomings if he insists on making his horse familiar with the place before the test. A show jumper is expected to enter the ring without such lengthy preparations.

Similar methods of judging to those just described, that is, with a preliminary and a principal test, were in use in Germany and in most other countries, although there was often one single score for both performances. The international dressage tests of the FEI, on the contrary, are judged in one single test. The various exercises are scored either separately or in groups, with marks from zero to ten. The sum of these marks gives the final results. The awarding of the prizes is preceded by a mere presentation of the riders in front of the public. There is no further possibility of changing the placings of the riders. So much for a broad outline of the two systems of judging.

It might be interesting to take a closer look at the individual performances seen at the old Austrian prize rides. The test was performed in a small arena of twenty to forty meters. The arena was laid out in such a way that the short side (twenty meters) might be lengthened to a stretch of a hundred meters. The original long side of forty meters thus became the short side of the larger arena. Since only the corners were marked, there was no difficulty in changing the small arena into the larger one. The judge's stand was on the short side of the small arena opposite the side where the riders entered.

After the major part of the preliminary test was performed in the small arena, the rest wound up in the larger arena. Exercises like circles, turns, voltes, changes of pace and tempo, lateral work, and halts were performed in the small arena. In the large arena the rider presented his horse at the extended canter once around the entire circumference (280 meters!), followed by two changes of the diagonal at the same tempo. In the Second and Third Levels the change of leg at the canter was executed through a few steps of medium trot at the center X. In the Fourth and Fifth Levels a flying change of lead was demanded. Immediately afterward the extended trot was performed around half the arena (140 meters) followed by a change over the diagonal at the same tempo. In a word, in the large arena the horse should demonstrate that after all the exercises at the collected tempo and in rapid succession in the small arena he had not lost the impulsion and forward urge expected from an all-purpose riding horse who may also be used in hunts and for cross-country expeditions. Here was an excellent trial for the correct and practical schooling of a riding horse. Moreover, it offered many a rider a chance to win over another contestant in spite of a relatively good performance if the latter's horse lacked the impulsion necessary in the large arena. It was an opportunity for any rider to give proof of the correct fundamental training of his horse according to the rules of classical horsemanship.

We should not turn away from knowledge approved by our elders and handed down through generations or consider it antiquated and out of date. Even mistakes or less applicable rules may become points of departure for reforms and improvements. Marking out a large arena nowadays might be a problem, though, for it is difficult to imagine a present-day horse show able to provide sufficient room. However, by periods at a brisk medium canter or by a longer duration of an extended trot with long strides many a mechanized horse whose training is nearer to the drilling of a poodle than to the classical concept of equitation might find his way back to Nature. We live in a time that brings the impossible within reach, so the solving of such problems should not present insurmountable difficulties. Dressage riding, which is so often misunderstood and misinterpreted, might then have a chance of being accepted in its true meaning by the general public.

At present there are two different systems of judging in use for dressage tests:

1. Combined judging
2. Separate judging

For combined judging the members of the jury sit together at a long table placed on the short side of the arena opposite the rider's entrance. At the end of the performance of each rider all of the judges decide the scores to be given. During the course of the test the president of the jury, in most instances, dictates to a secretary his remarks about the rider's performance. These remarks constitute the records which give the reasons for the scores awarded. Moreover, they contain advice for the rider to put to use in the further training of his horse. It cannot be emphasized too often that the records must be clear, comprehensible, and unequivocal in order to fulfill their purpose as a guideline for the rider. It frequently happens, however, that the records are nothing more than a maze of complicated technical terms and pompous phrases which are of no use to the rider and only confuse him.

The marks correspond to the regulations of the FEI with the following meaning:

10 excellent
9 very good
8 good
7 fairly good
6 satisfactory
5 sufficient
4 insufficient
3 fairly bad
2 bad
1 very bad
0 not performed

When evaluating a test, the judge compares the rider's presentation to a fictitious model performance to which he would confer the mark 10. The rider's scores will be higher or lower according to how close he comes to this image of perfection. The decisive point between better or worse lies between the marks 5 and 4. Here the judge must conscientiously determine whether the exercise deserves to be called sufficient or whether it is actually insufficient. However, he must not just hunt for faults but also courageously reward a truly good performance with a distinctly good mark. With the same conscientiousness he should give an inferior mark for an exercise poorly or carelessly performed. There are faint-hearted judges who never venture beyond the marks of five and six. This leads to the obvious conclusion that these judges lack equestrian knowledge or the courage of their opinion. Or both.

The method of combined judging is in general use in national horse shows for the First, Second, and Third Levels. There is a preliminary test including the jump in which each rider presents his horse individually. The principal test is ridden at a later time and before the public. Then the riders present their horses in a group either upon command or individually according to their planned routine. It goes without saying that equestrian tact requires that only those exercises be performed which were required in that particular class. During the principal test the jury has an ultimate opportunity to rectify, raise, or lower the marks according to the performances before their eyes.

In national horse shows the method of combined judging may also be applied to dressage tests of the Fourth and Fifth Levels. In this case, however, the placing is definitely decided in the preliminary test and the later "presentation" permits no alteration of the scores. This is the essential difference between a presentation and a principal test.

When the method of separate judging is applied, a platform about two feet high is placed at five meters' distance from the arena on the short side opposite the rider's entrance. Three tables are provided, one at the end of the center line for the president of the jury and the others at each end of the long sides of the arena for the two other judges. A secretary is placed at each judge's disposal to enter on the test sheets his remarks and the scores awarded. The tables for the jury are arranged in a similar manner for dressage tests of the FEI. In the case of a jury of five, the two additional judges are placed off the center of the long sides of the arena.

According to notes and records, the application of the method of separate judging in Austrian dressage riding may be traced back to the very beginnings of riding as a competitive sport. It was based on the achievements of

Austrian riders at the Concours Hippique in Turin in 1902, on the successes of General von Pongracz in "prize riding" in 1905 and 1910, on the victories at the international Concours Hippique in Frankfurt in 1910, when Austrian riders succeeded in placing first, third, fifth, sixth, and seventh in dressage in a field of twenty-six starters. The German hippological expert, Gustave Rau, in his book *International Equitation at the Olympic Games of 1936*, characterizes the equestrian standard by saying: "Austria, the stronghold of riding. . . ."

It might be worth taking a closer look at the application of the system of separate judging in Austria in those days. The jury was composed of three judges, all part of a group of well-known riders. They were either commanders of army training centers, successful competitors, or graduates of cavalry schools. The show grounds and the judges' stands were arranged as described earlier in this chapter. It was seen to that each judge remained undisturbed and uninfluenced from the outside. As a rule, the test of prize riding was composed of a preliminary and a principal test. The preliminary test, being the vital part of the class, offered the opportunity to judge each competitor individually and thoroughly. The scores of the preliminary test were decisive for the results. However, in case of severe faults during the principal test, changes in the final outcome were possible. Consequently, the judges were obliged to withhold the completed test sheets until the end of the principal test. As in today's scores, the marks ranged from ten to zero. According to the classes (First to Fifth Levels) there were fourteen to twenty spaces in the test sheets for the marks. This arrangement guided the judges as to the main points of the test. The sum of the marks in the test sheets gave the placing of the competitors according to the decision of each judge. The place numbers of all three judges were added up and the final winner determined. In other words, the winner of a test was not determined by adding the scores of the three judges but by adding their place numbers.

In the course of time the system of separate judging has taken precedence over that of combined judging. The FEI, for instance, resorted to this method of judging when dressage tests were first organized in its name and, by and large, has remained faithful to it. The changes that the method of separate judging has undergone in the course of over half a century will be discussed in detail in the following chapter. In several countries, such as Switzerland, Great Britain, Belgium, the Netherlands, the system of separate judging is most widely used, and it was introduced to the United States, Canada, Chile, Venezuela, and Argentina when the interest in dressage riding grew in those countries.

There are, of course, advantages and disadvantages to each method of judging. In combined judging, by the coordination of opinion of the three judges, a well-balanced and uniform evaluation of the rider's performance is made possible. Six eyes see better and more than two—a cogent point. Besides, the rider benefits from unanimous advice for the further training of his horse. The fact that the more experienced judge with greater authority is likely to assume a dominant position in the jury may have a positive effect. The other judges will profit from his experience and enlarge their knowledge and field of vision. This is especially valuable in the formation of young judges. However, this dominance may be tolerated only as long as it is not misused to overpower the decisions of the other judges. Or until it turns into bias toward a particular rider, either because he is a friend or for chauvinistic reasons.

The method of separate judging seems to be the appropriate means to give precedence to the personal opinion of each judge. When this method is applied, however, very often the judges are given an opportunity to correct their scores, as will be explained in the chapter about the Olympic Games. Any experiences and occurrences during the Olympic competitions, as the highest test in this discipline of the sport of riding, will produce repercussions on the organization of similar events on a national and international basis. After the Olympic Games in Munich in 1972, the cry for the method of open—not only separate —judging as already widely used in other sports with a similar mode of judging can no longer remain ignored. In open judging, the judge would have to own up to his decision immediately and publicly.

The demand for open judging is by no means new. As early as the beginning of the thirties, at the conference in Paris, the Austrian representative to the FEI, General von Pongracz, proposed the method of open judging with the scores made public immediately after each ride. A similar system was already in use in skating competitions. General von Pongracz had been an active rider from his earliest youth into advanced age. Well known in international jumping competitions, he had won the record for the high jump in 1913. His name was as well known in the dressage arena. In 1936 in Berlin at the age of seventy-two he placed sixteenth in a field of twenty-nine riders.

Repeatedly General von Pongracz brought his suggestion up before the assembled members of the FEI. Finally it was turned down with the explanation that in case of an erroneous judgement there might be demonstrations of displeasure from the public which would be detrimental to the sport of riding. The general was not the man to be put off with such shabby excuses. He declared in his stentorian voice: "The rider stands in the spotlight of public opinion. And so does the judge. The public has a right to express its opinion about any bad behaviour of a rider. In the same way it may stand up against an obviously unjust decision of a judge. In such a case it is of no interest whether the misjudgement springs from a lack of knowledge or from a weak character. A judge like that should be eliminated from the jury."

Before the Olympics of 1972 the method of open separate judging was tentatively applied several times although violently opposed by the supporters of "secretive" judging for rather obvious motives. Even after the close of the Olympics in Munich, the results of which will be discussed in Chapter 6, that particular group of judges advocated once again the return to the system of combined judging and especially to the opportunity for the judges to compare and adjust scores. This solution would be simple and easy, it is true, but it would in no way serve the cause of dressage riding. It would neither increase the interest of the general public nor help to preserve the supporters dressage has had so far. Only when the spectator can observe the performance and the evaluation of the ride in close sequence may he learn to form his own opinion and enlarge his knowledge. With the ride of the contestant and the scores simultaneously before his eyes he will be capable of greater understanding of the sport of riding.

The system of separate judging as practised in Munich in 1972 did not quite meet expectations. The results—the sum of forty-two marks—were made known after each rider had completed his test. Nevertheless, from the mere publication of the results very few spectators were able to obtain a clear picture of how these results were reached, or to assess the attitudes of the judges towards the principles of classical horsemanship and the regulations of the FEI. With our highly developed technology, however, it should be possible to announce the marks for the various groups of exercises publicly and immediately by way of luminous digits. Instead of putting down the marks on the test sheet the judge should make them visible on a large board by pressing the appropriate electric button. Such a technical device would immediately reveal the great differences of opinion among the various judges. This or similar systems of judging had already tentatively been put into practice in some horse shows. They are the only ones that deserve to be called "open judging."

It is understood that tradition must be respected and the principles of classical riding observed. But in the meantime we should not overlook a number of shortcomings in practical judging and close our eyes to the necessity of reforms. Injustice is a great wrong that few people are willing to suffer. Therefore, the general cry for justice will finally force those responsible in the various equestrian associations to take notice of the signs of grievance more or less openly expressed by the riders.

The verdicts in dressage tests—at the Olympic Games or in other international or national events—have in most cases through the years been unsatisfactory and sometimes even downright unavailing. Thereby misunderstanding between rider and judge has sprung up and

7. Lieutenant Count Rosen on Running Sister—Bronze medal 1920
8. Mr. Olson on Günstling—Bronze medal 1928

9. Major Lesage on Taine — Gold medal 1932 (Bronze medal 1924 on Plumarol)

10. Major Marion on Linon— Silver medal 1928 and 1932

11. Captain Tuttle on Olympic—Bronze medal 1932

12. First Lieutenant Pollay on Kronos—Gold medal 1936
13. Major Gerhard on Absinth—Silver medal 1936

the gap has deepened ever since. The general public in most instances cannot follow the judge's ideas either.

The understanding between rider and judge must suffer if the judge does not have to stand up for his decision openly in front of the general public. Dressage riding as a whole is not benefited by this situation. Judging dressage does not mean just to state a verdict about a rider but to give guidelines for this work. This cannot be underlined too often. In most cases, however, the decisions of the different judges point in opposite directions, making it impossible for the rider to gain any useful advice. He must be resigned to the fact that his painstaking work through many years is simply being scored—no more. It has happened before that many a talented rider in exasperation turned away from dressage riding and took up show jumping. In this branch of riding it is plain what is expected from him and the meaning cannot be twisted. It is small wonder that many of today's young riders prefer to concentrate on show jumping. Not only does this sport require less intense time and work and patience but also —and above all—it is decided by clear and unequivocal judgements, understandable to the general public as well.

There is no doubt that the office of judging as well as the judges themselves have forfeited part of their authority by recurrent misjudgements. Whether these erroneous judgements were due to inadequate knowledge or to partiality is of no interest. A judge of this sort, in either case, is out of place on the show grounds. Conclusions must be drawn from this knowledge. A person placed in public light is responsible to public opinion, the judge as well as the rider. As the rider may be disqualified for an insufficient performance—as, for instance, when his horse refuses a jump three times or when in dressage he repeatedly comes off course or scores zero with his performance —so should the judge be eliminated whose verdict is in flagrant contradiction to those of the other judges. Provided, of course, he is not capable of giving unequivocal reasons for his decisions. A tribunal should be established before which a judge has to appear and explain his reasons.

My words may sound uncompromising but they are dictated by the ardent desire, in the interest of dressage riding, to establish or restore the authority and superiority of the dressage judge which may only be gained and preserved by absolute impartiality and perfect command of the subject. It has been said repeatedly that the judge is not to give scores only but also set guidelines for the rider's future work. This is easily said but difficult to put into practice, for it presupposes that the judge has a thorough knowledge of the subject. And this is why the judge must have been a rider himself. On principle, it should be required that the judge of a dressage competition must himself be or have been able to perform in the saddle what he is called upon to judge in others. It should be possible to find a sufficient number of suitable judges among the numerous successful dressage riders who have proved their knowledge and abilities. It seems that with a little good will a solution might be found. In many cases, judging dressage has become the domain of certain closed circles which exercise some sort of dictatorship, seemingly infallible and bent upon defending their position. Self-interest is given precedence over universal interest, unfortunately at the expense of the sport of riding.

A rider installed in the judge's stand can fully enter into a rider's feelings and imagine the conflict imposed on a practising athlete by an unjust verdict. Many a judge, were he nearer to active riding himself, would judge with greater care and conscientiousness. He would have a deeper understanding of the bitterness caused by an incomprehensible decision.

Consequently, any efforts to encourage the rising generation of judges should be supported energetically by the official boards. Not every rider will necessarily become a good judge, but he fulfills the essential requirements for the task. The point is to provide the opportunity for him to enlarge his experience and knowledge. In national horse shows the young judges-to-be should be assigned functions that enable them to become familiar with the activities of a judge. They might work as secretaries, sit next to the judge as an observer, or judge for the first time as auxiliary judges together with an experienced man. The method of combined judging seems to be particularly appropriate for introducing a young judge to his office. Hearing the record being dictated teaches him to use his eyes to see and his mind to evaluate the rider's performance correctly. The practical phase of schooling the rising generation of judges should be a basis to be supplemented by theoretical seminars organized by the national federations. Comprehensive knowledge of the literature on the subject of the training of horse and rider is a vital part of the mental equipment of the future judge.

# 6

# The Grand Prix de Dressage and Judging at the Olympic Games 1912 to 1968

The resolutions of the FEI as the top organization of the sport of riding influence the regulations of the national federations. There is an endeavour to co-ordinate various systems of the sport indigenous to the different nations. Other regulations are obligatory for all countries. In particular, all changes decided by the FEI concerning the program of the dressage tests as well as the methods of judging dressage competitions must be respected by the national federations. In view of this fact it is worth-while to point out and discuss critically the difficulties that have arisen in judging the most difficult dressage test, the Grand Prix, from the inception of equestrian events on to the program of the Olympic Games.

The world's athletes will forever be indebted to the energy and youthful enthusiasm of the Frenchman Pierre de

Coubertin, at whose instigation the ancient Olympic Games, held from 776 B.C. to A.D. 393, were revived in Athens in 1896 and continued in events of the same kind every four years up to the present day. The sole interruptions were the two World Wars. And the riders among us should keep in mind that it was the Swedish Count Clarence von Rosen who succeeded in having the three equestrian events, the Combined Training, the Grand Prix de Dressage, and the jumping included in the program of the Olympic Games for the first time in Stockholm in 1912.

Some recent statements contradict the prevailing opinion that equestrian competitions were not introduced into the Olympic Games until 1912 by citing events as early as 1900 held in Paris with as many as three jumping classes in which representatives of four countries participated. The question remains, however, whether this equestrian event was part of the Olympic Games or was connected with the World Exposition in Paris which took place at the same time.*

Significantly the programs of the Olympics that followed indicate nothing about any participation of riders. Moreover, Count Rosen's endeavour to have equestrian events accepted in the program remained unsuccessful also in London in 1908.

It is with gratitude that we riders think of the Swedish count who has made a place for our sport in the great fes-

---

* The questionable sporting standard of that obscurely interlaced double event was characterized by Professor Carl Diem, renowned expert on the Olympics, in his *World History of Sport and Physical Exercise*: "The Olympic Games of 1900 may be found in our lists. But in reality they were not Olympic Games but part of an entertainment program. Besides, no official report gives details about those Games. What was presented was a monster program which indiscriminately mingled amateur competitions with world championships and professional contests."

tival of the world's youth. Acknowledging his achievement is not enough, though. Rather should we try to find new ways and ideas to improve the systems of dressage competitions and the methods of judging by taking a close look at the dressage tests and their results at the successive Olympic Games.

Sixty-two riders from ten nations participated in the equestrian events of the Fifth Olympic Games in Stockholm in 1912: Belgium, Chile, Denmark, France, Germany, Great Britain, Norway, Russia, Sweden, and the U.S.A.

Twenty-one riders of eight nations competed in the individual contest of the Grand Prix de Dressage. The following riders placed:
1. Captain Count Bonde (Sweden) on Emperor
2. Major Boltenstern (Sweden) on Neptun
3. Lieutenant von Blixen-Finecke (Sweden) on Maggie
Medals for the teams in this discipline were not awarded before 1928.

Seven nations with twenty-seven riders participated in the Combined Training. The teams placed as follows:
1. Sweden, 2. Germany, 3. U.S.A.
In jumping, six nations with twenty-three riders started. The teams of Sweden, France, and Germany won first, second, and third places respectively.

In view of the subject of this book, the main interest is with the dressage competitions. Therefore, with both the Combined Training and the jumping only the places of the teams are noted and those of the individual contests are disregarded. But there is one competitor of 1912 who should be remembered for a special reason. Considering the decisive role of the American General George S. Patton, Jr., in saving the Spanish Riding School and the

Lipizzaner stud farm in the chaotic spring days of 1945, it is of valid interest that then Lieutenant Patton participated in the pentathlon of the Olympic Games in Stockholm in 1912.

The Games of the 7th Olympiad in Anvers in 1920 saw ninety participants of eight nations in the equestrian competitions: Belgium, Finland, France, Italy, Netherlands, Norway, Sweden, and the U.S.A. The medals of the Grand Prix de Dressage for which five nations with seventeen riders competed were awarded to:

1. Captain Lundblad (Sweden) on Uno
2. Lieutenant Sandström (Sweden) on Sabel
3. Lieutenant Count Rosen (Sweden) on Running Sister

Twenty-five riders of seven nations competed in the Combined Training won by the teams of: 1. Sweden, 2. Italy, 3. Belgium.

The jumping, in which six nations participated with twenty-seven riders, was won by the teams of: 1. Sweden, 2. Belgium, 3. Italy.

Thanks to the activity of the Fédération Equestre Internationale (FEI), founded in 1921, the equestrian contest at the 8th Olympic Games in Paris in 1924 received fresh impetus which became obvious in the number of participants as well as in the tests themselves. There were ninety-nine riders of eighteen nations: Austria, Belgium, Bulgaria, Czechoslovakia, Denmark, Finland, France, Great Britain, Italy, Netherlands, Norway, Poland, Portugal, Spain, Sweden, Switzerland, the U.S.A., and Yugoslavia.

In the Grand Prix de Dressage twenty-four riders represented nine nations. The medals were awarded to:

1. General Linder (Sweden) on Piccolomini
2. First Lieutenant Sandström (Sweden) on Sabel

3. Captain Lesage (France) on Plumarol

The medals of the Combined Training went to the teams of: 1. Netherlands, 2. Sweden, 3. Italy. Forty-four riders of twelve nations participated.

In the jumping contested by eleven nations with forty-three riders the winning teams were: 1. Sweden, 2. Switzerland, 3. Portugal.

The increase in number as well as in standard persisted in the 9th Olympics. In the equestrian competition in Amsterdam in 1928 twenty nations participated with 114 riders: Argentina, Austria, Belgium, Bulgaria, Czechoslovakia, Denmark, Finland, France, Germany, Hungary, Italy, Japan, Netherlands, Norway, Poland, Portugal, Spain, Sweden, Switzerland, and the U.S.A.

In the Grand Prix de Dressage in which twelve nations participated with thirty riders the medals went to the individual rides of:

1. Baron von Langen (Germany) on Draufgänger
2. Major Marion (France) on Linon
3. Mr. Olsen (Sweden) on Günstling

The teams of seventeen nations with forty-six riders entered the Combined Training and placed as follows: 1. Netherlands, 2. Norway, 3. Sweden.

It seems worth mentioning that the winner of the Grand Prix de Dressage participated also in the stadium jumping; that one rider competed in the Grand Prix as well as in the Combined Training; and four others rode in the Combined Training and the stadium jumping.

At the Games in Los Angeles in 1932 only six nations with thirty-one riders participated in the equestrian events: France, Japan, Mexico, Netherlands, Sweden, and the U.S.A. The individual medals of the Grand Prix de

Dressage, ten riders of four nations, competing, went to:
1. Major Lesage (France) on Taine
2. Major Marion (France) on Linon
3. Captain Tuttle (U.S.A.) on Olympic
The team medals were awarded to: 1. France, 2. Sweden,
3. U.S.A.

In the Three-Day Event the teams of five nations with thirteen riders scored as follows: 1. U.S.A., 2. Netherlands. The third medal was not awarded.

Only four nations with twelve riders competed in the stadium jumping. Therefore, the team medal was not awarded. The individual medals went to:
1. Lieutenant Nishi (Japan) on Uranus
2. Major Chamberlain (U.S.A.) on Show Girl
3. Lieutenant Count Rosen (Sweden) on Empire

It was in Los Angeles that for the first time during the Olympic equestrian competitions an incident occurred as a result of the absolutely incomprehensible decision of the attending representative of the FEI. In the course of the reorganization and promotion of equestrian competitions with respect to the increase of standards for the dressage tests as well as changes of details in the system of judging, the competitors were particularly checked for the prohibited use of audible aids. There could be no objection to that, for the application of invisible and inaudible aids is one of the principles of classical horsemanship. However, it is hard to understand why a rider should be disqualified from the individual competition because of the use of the tongue if at the same time and in spite of this fault his performance is counted with the results of his team and he and his teammates are awarded the silver medal. Presumably an entire team should not lose a medal because of the questionable testimony of an eavesdropper posted at the edge of the arena. This might be the only possible explanation for this very strange decision. Such inconsistent evaluation at a contest is certainly not an honourable page in the annals of the Olympic Games.

At the Games in Berlin in 1936 the equestrian competitions reached their highest standard before the Second World War with respect both to the number of contestants and to the degree of difficulties in the Grand Prix de Dressage. One hundred and thirty-three riders of twenty-one nations entered in these competitions: Austria, Belgium, Bulgaria, Czechoslovakia, Denmark, Finland, France, Germany, Great Britain, Hungary, Italy, Japan, Netherlands, Norway, Poland, Portugal, Rumania, Sweden, Switzerland, Turkey, and the U.S.A.

In the Grand Prix eleven nations (Austria, Czechoslovakia, Denmark, France, Germany, Hungary, Netherlands, Norway, Sweden, Switzerland, and the U.S.A.) had entered nine teams of three riders. There were two individual riders, making altogether twenty-nine riders. The individual medals were awarded to:

1. First Lieutenant Pollay (Germany) on Kronos
2. Major Gerhard (Germany) on Absinth
3. Major Podhajsky (Austria) on Nero

The teams placed as follows: 1. Germany, 2. France, 3. Sweden.

In the Combined Training fourteen nations participated with teams of three riders and five nations with eight individual riders, totaling fifty riders in all. The team medals were won by: 1. Germany, 2. Poland, 3. Great Britain. Fifty-four riders of eighteen nations with three riders each contested the stadium jumping in which the following teams placed: 1. Germany, 2. Netherlands, 3. Portugal.

Attention should be called to the fact that one rider participated in the Grand Prix de Dressage as well as in the Combined Training; another in the Grand Prix and in the stadium jumping. Four riders started in the Combined Training as well as in the stadium jumping.

As I have participated in Grand Prix tests both as a rider and as a judge, I want to enlarge the present description of the dressage competitions at the Olympic Games by discussing in detail the tests required, the methods of judging, and several incidents that occurred, beginning with 1936, which is the year of my first Olympic Games.

Shortly before 1936, the FEI decided upon the dressage test at the Concours de Dressage, later European Championship or Concours de Dressage International Officiel (CDIO). At the Concours de Dressage they consisted of a Prix St. George as a less difficult preparatory test and of the Grand Prix. The same Grand Prix was used to determine the medalists at the Olympic Games. Sometime later a test "in between," the Intermédiare, was added to the preparatory test, and the Grand Prix at the Olympic contests was completed by the ride-off which decided the outcome of the test. At the beginning, the FEI tests were called out, as was the custom with all dressage classes. At international horse shows and the Olympic Games, consequently, interpreters had to be employed. From the early thirties onward, however, the experiences gained on that subject resulted in the rule that the required test was to be ridden from memory.

This new regulation was by no means unanimously applauded by the active riders for whom it meant addi-

tional stress and diverted concentration. When riding a
test by heart the rider no longer concentrates entirely on
his horse but must constantly think of the sequence of exercises which, with the great number of figures and the
changes of tempo and pace, presents serious problems. As
a consequence, riders went off course quite frequently, as
they still do, for which penal points are administered.
There were even grotesque incidents, as for instance
when a president of the judging jury, despite his ample
experience, simply missed a rider's mistake in the course.
He realized the mistake only after a series of other exercises, although he should have followed the performance
with the aid of the score sheet. Thus he failed in his responsibility as a judge. For it is among the duties of a
judge to interrupt the rider immediately by ringing a bell
and telling him where to begin to repeat the test. Unpleasant discussions of all sorts were the outcome of such
incidents.

Furthermore, learning the test by heart causes the rider
to repeat it far too often during training. This may easily
lead to mechanizing his horse, a dangerous direction for a
rider to take and one that must be condemned from the
point of view of serious schooling.

As already noted, the requirements made of the dressage riders were increased from one Olympics to the next
and reached a climax in the 1936 Games, when movements of Haute Ecole such as pirouettes, flying changes at
each stride, piaffe, and passage were included in the program. I want to underline particularly that this dressage
test did justice to the principles of classical riding in
every respect, allowing sufficient space for the basic requirements expected from a dressage horse such as the
purity of the paces, impulsion, suppleness, and so on. It

should be mentioned especially that the rider was to guide his horse with the reins in one hand during some of the exercises. It was clear that this test was not designed by a rider in theory but by men who themselves were capable of practically demonstrating on horseback what they expected from other riders. This fact became obvious in the structure of the test.

There was an artistic concept in the lay-out of the different exercises. They succeeded each other in harmonious sequence from which no tension might arise and which at the same time offered the judge opportunity to examine thoroughly the standard of horse and rider. It is small wonder that even years afterward experts still stated that the dressage test of the Olympic Games of 1936 was the best designed so far.

The members of the jury were increased to five in number. They sat together with their auxiliary judges at a long table on the short side of the arena opposite the rider's entrance. They were not separated from each other in any way. The performance of the rider was to be judged with the marks from ten to zero and in thirty-nine individual scores. The rider had seventeen minutes to complete his routine. This space of time was ample for any horse going forward with impulsion. There were few contestants who received penal points for exceeding time.

The marks in sixteen groups of exercises were multiplied by the coefficient 5, of fourteen others by 10, of two more by 15, of five by 20 and of two by 30. The coefficient was introduced to take into account the varying degrees of difficulty, with higher scores rewarding the more difficult exercises. There were positive and negative sides to this method. It was certainly of great disadvantage if a judge lost the thread of his general evaluation and was surprised and dissatisfied with his own verdict when the result of his scores was published by the scoring office. Besides, during great international competitions it happened on several occasions that chauvinistic judges skillfully awarded higher scores to the riders of their own country when there was a high coefficient and lower ones to those competitors who might become dangerous rivals. In justifying themselves they might point out that they had given high marks, too, to the great adversaries of their nation. However, a close look would reveal that the high marks were mostly to be found where there were low coefficients. In controversies following the Olympic Games of 1936 the application of the coefficient has been contested on many occasions. However, since then it has been applied in varying manners.

As is the rule, after each ride the scores in the test sheets were evaluated by the scoring office and the placing of each rider determined. The rider with the highest scores placed first, the last being the rider with the lowest scores. The sum of the place marks of all five judges gave the result of the competition. The test was won by the rider with the lowest place marks, and the other riders were placed according to the scale of their place marks. The case of two riders with identical place marks was decided by the higher scores. A ride-off was provided in the event that two or more riders obtained identical places together with the identical total scores. A special test was to be ridden in that case, which, however, has not occurred so far in any Olympic Games or International Concours de Dressage.

The system of ranging the contestants by way of place marks is applied to other fields of sport as well. It limits the judge's chance to manipulate the decisions of his colleagues by biased evaluation with disproportionate scores for those contestants whom he wants to see in the top places. All this can happen if the results of the score sheets alone decide the test. When evaluating according to the system of place marks, on the contrary, the judge can at the very best help one rider by awarding him the highest marks. But he has no chance of influencing the decisions of the other judges. For the sake of impartiality, the evaluation according to place marks should by all means be maintained.

The rider and the observer are primarily interested in knowing the order in which each judge ranged the competitors. It is not easily ascertained by the score sheets alone. On the contrary, this system prevents the observer from recognizing the large differences in the scores of the individual judges in the first instance. Could it be on purpose?

After the Olympic Games in 1936 it was planned—and in part put into practice—that the highest as well as the lowest scores of each of the five judges of the jury would be eliminated. Furthermore, at the Concours de Dressage in Berlin in July 1937, as an experiment, each rider had to present his horse to the judges on two consecutive days, a procedure similar to that of the Prix des Nations of the jumping riders. The result was announced after the second ride and was based on the sum of the scores of both tests. This attempt points to the understandable wish of the judges to see the riders a second time and then only to decide the definite places. It offers a better opportunity to the judge to compare the different performances, especially of a large group of competitors. There were pros and cons to these procedures, some from the point of view of organization. Before they could be further developed and tested, however, they were overrun by the political events leading up to the Second World War and its aftermath.

The vital importance of reforming the entire system of judging dressage classes in general as well as the Olympic tests in particular becomes obvious when a close look is taken at the verdicts of the judges at the Olympic Games in Berlin. Every one of the five judges had one or more compatriots among the competitors. Three judges placed their countrymen first, three placed them second. One rider who was placed second by his fellow countryman ranked seventeenth, twentieth, and twice in the twenty-first place in the scores of the four other judges. This was in a group of twenty-nine contestants from eleven nations! Any further comment is superfluous.

The first Olympic Games after the Second World War were held in London in 1948. Seventeen nations delegated 103 riders to the equestrian events: Argentina, Austria, Brazil, Denmark, Finland, France, Great Britain, Ireland, Italy, Mexico, Netherlands, Portugal, Spain, Sweden, Switzerland, Turkey, and the U.S.A.

Nine nations (Argentina, Austria, France, Mexico, Portugal, Spain, Sweden, Switzerland, and the U.S.A.) with five teams of three riders plus four individual riders—a total of nineteen riders—participated in the Grand Prix de Dressage. The individual medals were won by:

1. Captain Moser (Switzerland) on Hummer
2. Colonel Joussaume (France) on Harpagon
3. Captain Boltenstern (Sweden) on Trumpf

The teams placed: 1. Sweden, 2. France, 3. the U.S.A.

The team medals of the Combined Training went to: 1. the U.S.A., 2. Sweden, 3. Mexico. There were forty-five riders, sixteen nations competing with fourteen teams of three riders plus three individual competitors. The stadium jumping had fourteen teams of three riders from fifteen nations and two individual riders, forty-four riders in all. The following teams placed: 1. Mexico, 2. Spain, 3. Great Britain.

Four riders competed in both the Grand Prix de Dressage and the Combined Training, and one rider in the Combined Training and the stadium jumping.

Thirteen minutes were provided for the dressage test, which was to be scored for twenty-one groups of exercises. As always the scores went from ten to zero. The influence of the coefficient was considerably decreased, six marks being multiplied by 5, twelve by 10, one by 15, and one by 20.

The equestrian standard had sunk to an alarmingly low level as a result of the war. In Berlin in 1936 the horses had not only performed the most difficult exercises brilliantly but had also excelled in the regularity and harmony of all paces. In London, none of this was to be seen although the test had been made considerably easier by eliminating piaffe and passage. And what followed? The subterfuge of a "modern concept" was invented, the ideal of which was presumably to have horses that jogged along without regularity and cadence.

The jury was reduced to three judges. Two of them placed their compatriots first and second. The third judge had only one rider from his nation and he gave him first place by awarding scores out of all proportion. One rider who had been placed second by his compatriot was put in eighth and tenth places in a field of nineteen riders from nine nations by the two other judges.

It was hard to understand why the number of judges was reduced from five to three. A larger jury would have in any case guaranteed a more impartial judgement. A grotesque explanation was given for eliminating place marks, namely that the system of deciding the winner by such marks was not applicable with a jury of three judges. This decision, which was made public at the very last moment, in fact gave one of the judges the chance to give the gold medal to his compatriot whose place mark was nine, while a better rider with the place mark eight had to content himself with the bronze medal.

There were great hue and cry and criticism. But the judges or the responsible organization had taken care to prevent all outsiders from having a glimpse behind the scenes. Against all laws of fairness the names of the judges remained a secret even for many months after the Games and in the lists and official reports were supplanted by A, B, and C.

The negative incidents just mentioned did not remain without influence, as will be seen in the discussion of the Olympic Games that followed. Meanwhile, after those 1948 Games, Argentina, which had delegated teams to all three equestrian events, declared on leaving London that the country would not participate in Olympic dressage tests until the system of judging was reformed. And in fact there were no Argentine dressage riders at the 1952 Games in Helsinki.

The equestrian events of the Helsinki Games saw twenty-five nations with 138 riders start: Argentina, Brazil, Bulgaria, Canada, Chile, Denmark, Egypt, Finland, France, Germany, Great Britain, Ireland, Italy, Japan, Mexico, Netherlands, Norway, Portugal, Rumania, South Korea, Spain, Sweden, Switzerland, the U.S.A., and the U.S.S.R.

There were ten nations (Chile, Denmark, France, Germany, Norway, Portugal, Sweden, Switzerland, the U.S.A. and the U.S.S.R.) with eight teams of three riders and three individual riders, that is, twenty-seven riders in the Grand Prix de Dressage. The individual medals went to:

1. Major St. Cyr (Sweden) on Master Rufus
2. Lis Hartel (Denmark) on Jubilee
3. Colonel Joussaume (France) on Harpagon

The team medals went to: 1. Sweden, 2. Switzerland, 3. Germany.

Fifty-nine riders of twenty-one nations with nineteen teams of three riders and two individual riders started in the Combined Training. The teams of Sweden, Germany, and the U.S.A. placed first, second, and third.

Twenty nations with sixteen teams of three riders and four individual riders participated in the stadium jumping, that is fifty-two riders. The following teams placed: 1. Great Britain, 2. Chile, 3. the U.S.A.

One rider participating in the Grand Prix also competed in the stadium jumping. One competitor started in the Combined Training as well as in jumping; another Three-Day-Event contestant was to participate in the stadium jumping but missed the start.

At the 1952 Olympics the Grand Prix was again raised to the level of Olympic standards by reintroducing piaffe and passage. The test was judged by a jury of five, with the highest and the lowest scores dropped. Consequently, the scores of three judges only counted for the final results. The place marks were not taken into consideration and have not been reintroduced since. Instead, after each ride the judges compared the marks they had given for the different groups of exercises in the test. The scores had to be corrected in case of a difference exceeding four marks. The test sheet provided a special column for these corrections. As a logical consequence to this procedure, the judge with the greatest experience and knowledge but also with an overpowering personality forced his opinion upon the other members of the jury. Moreover, weak and uncertain judges, by wavering between the indifferent marks four to seven, escaped having to stand up for their evaluations to the president of the jury. All in all, this was certainly not a satisfactory solution of the problem.

Again the scores of the judges were unfortunately revealed to be of doubtful value. Three of the five judges had compatriots to evaluate and promptly placed them first, although with the other judges they landed in the ninth, eleventh, and nineteenth places. Two judges awarded the second place to their fellow countrymen, one of whom placed twentieth with one of the other judges, and that in a field of twenty-seven competitors from ten nations!

The dressage riders of the Olympic Games in 1952 displayed a better standard of riding than those of 1948. Nevertheless, their performances were still far inferior to those of the Olympics of 1936. Above all, an alarming difference of conception manifested itself among the judges. It was reflected in their evaluations, which were justifiably criticised and even disputed. Having closely followed the Grand Prix de Dressage from the first to the last rider, the observer could not help but shake his head at the score sheets of the different judges. The lack of any clearly defined opinion and set of standards became aggravatingly obvious. It was hard to imagine what actual ideal of a dressage horse the members of the jury might have in mind. It is true that everything that had been expounded about the modern conception of dressage in

1948 seemed to have been forgotten. But now there was neither any apparent new train of thought nor a return to the principles of classical horsemanship.

Incidentally but curiously, in Helsinki the representatives of the so-called Romanic school rode partly with a very strong contact with the bit, almost giving the impression that they forced their horses' heads into a certain position by means of the reins. The representatives of the so-called Germanic school, on the contrary, showed their horses on a long, sometimes even slack, rein. Such observations prove once more that one should not speak about a Germanic or a Romanic style of riding and even less relate them to a firm or light contact with the bit. This is ridiculous and irrelevant.

At the equestrian events of the Games in June 1956 in Stockholm, twenty-nine nations with 158 riders participated in the equestrian events: Argentina, Australia, Austria, Belgium, Brazil, Bulgaria, Cambodia, Canada, Denmark, Egypt, Finland, France, Germany, Great Britain, Hungary, Ireland, Italy, Japan, Netherlands, Norway, Portugal, Rumania, Spain, Sweden, Switzerland, Turkey, the U.S.A., the U.S.S.R., and Venezuela.

Seventeen nations (Argentina, Austria, Bulgaria, Canada, Denmark, Finland, France, Germany, Great Britain, Netherlands, Norway, Portugal, Rumania, Sweden, Switzerland, the U.S.A., and the U.S.S.R.) with eight teams of three riders and twelve individual riders, that is, thirty-six riders, competed in the Grand Prix de Dressage. The individual medals were won by:

1. Major St. Cyr (Sweden) on Juli
2. Lis Hartel (Denmark) on Jubilee
3. Liselott Linsenhoff (Germany) on Adular

The teams placed: 1. Sweden, 2. Germany, 3. Switzerland.

In the Combined Training nineteen nations with teams of three riders each participated, fifty-seven riders in all. The team medals went to: 1. Great Britain, 2. Germany, 3. Canada.

The stadium jumping was contested by twenty-four nations with nineteen teams of three riders and eight individual riders, altogether sixty-five participants. The team medals were won by: 1. Germany, 2. Italy, 3. Great Britain.

The equestrian events in Stockholm in 1956 were the first and so far the only ones to be separated from the rest of the program of the Olympic Games. In that year the Olympics were held in Melbourne, Australia, where the quarantine regulations rendered the participation of horses impossible. Sweden magnanimously offered the 1912 Olympic stadium and thus secured the participation of riders in the 16th Olympiad. The setting created especially for these competitions together with the solemn ceremonies were so impressive that the majority of those present remember the 1956 equestrian games in Stockholm as a unique experience.

The degree of difficulty of the dressage test was increased by adding different exercises to the program of the 1952 Olympic Games. There were flying changes on the circle, for instance, beginning with two four-time changes, decreasing to two changes after each stride, and increasing again to two changes after four strides. This exercise on the circle was highly criticised by some riders who called it a circus trick. However, its performance should be no problem for any dressage horse schooled by the principles of classical equitation, possessing sufficient

balance and suppleness, and taking a perfect contact with
the bit.

In this test there were for the first time no coefficients,
which had been employed since 1936 in varying degrees.
In spite of retaining the system of comparison of scores,
there were a number of discrepancies which are discussed
below and which seriously jeopardized the future of the
sport of dressage.

The behaviour of the jury was in flagrant contradiction
to the positive efforts of the organizers. Two of the five
judges had no countrymen competing in this test. Two of
the other judges considered for medals only their own
compatriots, whom they placed first, second, and third,
while with the other judges their scores did not amount to
more than the eighth, fifteenth, nineteenth, and twenty-
third places. Most aggravating of all, this happened although for the first time the judges had sworn the Olympic oath for fair and impartial judging! The fifth judge
awarded the first place to a contestant from his country
while he placed the two other compatriots somewhere in
the middle of a field of thirty-six riders from seventeen
nations.

These incidents at the dressage test in Stockholm
aroused general indignation, so much so that the International Olympic Committee was about to eliminate the
dressage test altogether from the Olympic Games, an idea
that had been considered for some time. Due to the initia-
tive of the president of the Fédération Equestre Internationale, H.R.H. Prince Bernhard of the Netherlands, it
was possible to ward off this serious blow to the art of riding. Energetic measures were taken on one side and on
the other there was readiness to compromise. The two
guiltiest dressage judges were barred for life from any

further international activity, and each nation was allowed to delegate only two riders to the Olympics in Rome, thereby eliminating any team medals.

In the equestrian events of the Rome Olympics in September 1960, one hundred and fifty-two riders of twenty-nine nations participated: Argentina, Australia, Austria, Belgium, Brazil, Bulgaria, Canada, Czechoslovakia, Denmark, Egypt, France, Germany, Great Britain, Hungary, Ireland, Italy, Japan, New Zealand, Poland, Portugal, Rumania, South Korea, Spain, Sweden, Switzerland, Turkey, Uruguay, the U.S.A., and the U.S.S.R. In the Grand Prix de Dressage, ten nations (Argentina, Bulgaria, Czechoslovakia, Germany, Great Britain, Portugal, Sweden, Switzerland, the U.S.A., and the U.S.S.R.) were present with seventeen riders. As stated, the number of participants in the dressage test was limited to two riders per nation. The medals were won by:

1. Filatow (U.S.S.R.) on Absent
2. Fischer (Switzerland) on Wald
3. Neckermann (Germany) on Asbach

Nineteen nations with seventy-three riders were delegated to the Combined Training with the teams placing as follows: 1. Australia, 2. Switzerland, 3. France.

The jumping was organized in two separate contests. The individual jumping was held on two courses at the Piazza di Siena. The team jumping—Prix des Nations—was ridden in the Olympic stadium. Eighteen nations participated with fifty-four riders, and medals went to: 1. Germany, 2. U.S.A., 3. Italy.

The dressage test was somewhat altered and the time allowed was twelve minutes. Thirty-three groups of exercises had to be evaluated. As an innovation the following

Collective Marks were introduced, which at the end of the ride were also to be scored by ten to zero.

1. Paces (regularity and freedom)
2. Impulsion
3. Submission, suppleness, and lightness of the horse
4. Position, seat of the rider, correct use of the aids

To a limited degree the coefficients were reintroduced, that is, the coefficient 2 in seven groups of exercises, including practically all of the airs of the Haute Ecole such as piaffe, pirouettes, and half pass at the canter. The coefficient 3 was awarded for flying changes at the canter at every stride, for the lightness of the horse, and for the rider's seat and use of the aids. One coefficient of 4 was administered for the Collective Mark given for regularity and freedom of the paces.

Another innovation was the ride-off in which 25 per cent of the highest placed riders rode the test for a second time. The final result was deducted from the sum of the scores of both tests. Moreover, films were made of each rider and consulted by the judges before deciding the scores in order to correct their marks if necessary. This was a rather complicated procedure in theory and in practice it had disastrous consequences.

The equestrian standard was of no extraordinary level to begin with. In addition, due to the small entry of only seventeen competitors in an Olympic event together with the complicated system of judging, the interest of the public died down alarmingly. During the test the otherwise overcrowded grandstands began to thin out. The last riders presented their horses in front of rows of empty seats. The results were not published until four days later. This retarded publication and the placements, which were incomprehensible to the experts and to most persons interested in the Grand Prix de Dressage, caused a great deal of justified criticism in the international press.

In these Olympic Games three judges assessed the work of years of the best international dressage riders. They came from countries that had not delegated any contestants to the Grand Prix de Dressage. The entire system of judging was surrounded by incredible anonymity. By roundabout means, it was heard that in a special conference the judges consulted films made for that purpose before deciding the final places of the riders. No wonder that the definite results were not made known until four days later. It was a hopeless system which had no place in Olympic Games.

Another innovation was the side judge, who, as an observer, was to advise the jury from his point of view whenever disagreements arose. However, he was not authorized to give scores. But again this was not a satisfactory solution to the problem. Nevertheless, the office of the side judge was maintained up to the Games of 1968.

The Games of the 18th Olympiad took place in October 1964 in Tokyo. Thus the long-time Japanese aspiration was at last fulfilled to make up for the cancellation of plans to hold the Games there in 1940. Twenty nations (Argentina, Australia, Brazil, Canada, Chile, France, Germany, Great Britain, Ireland, Italy, Japan, Mexico, New Zealand, Portugal, South Korea, Spain, Sweden, Switzerland, the U.S.A., and the U.S.S.R.) delegated one hundred and fifteen riders to the equestrian events in Tokyo. The Grand Prix de Dressage was contested by nine nations (Argentina, Canada, Germany, Great Britain, Japan, Sweden, Switzerland, the U.S.A., and the U.S.S.R.) with six teams of three riders and four individual riders, altogether 22 riders. The individual winners were:

1. Chammartin (Switzerland) on Woermann
2. Boldt (Germany) on Remus
3. Filatow (U.S.S.R.) on Absent

The team medals were won by 1. Germany, 2. Switzerland, 3. U.S.S.R.

Twelve nations with forty-eight riders participated in the Combined Training. The teams ranged: 1. Italy, 2. U.S.A., 3. Germany.

Fourteen teams of three riders and three individual riders, that is, forty-five riders, started in the Prix des Nations. The medals were won by the teams of: 1. Germany, 2. France, 3. Italy.

There were insignificant changes in the test of the Grand Prix and the coefficients were limited to the Collective Marks. The time of the ride was not to exceed twelve and a half minutes. The jury consisted of three judges. Separated from each other, they were to evaluate thirty-two groups of exercises with marks from ten to zero. Again the scores were examined by the president of the jury, who ordered them to be corrected if the comparison revealed gross divergencies. The four Collective Marks, three of which were multiplied by the coefficient 2 and one by 3, were determined by the group. Corrections in the test sheets and the final marks given collectively more or less annulled the idea of separate judging.

In a ride-off the judges evaluated the better 25 per cent of the participants for a second time. The scores of both rides were added up to determine the final results and the winners of the individual medals. The side judge was again an observer without a vote. The same system was maintained in Mexico in 1968. Since in Tokyo, too, the judges saw films made of each rider before making a final decision, the publication of the results was delayed by days. Again it was a rather un-Olympic procedure.

Because of the distance of the Games from my homeland, I could not be present and form a personal opinion. It was not easy to obtain an unbiased over-all view from the various contradicting reports. They were either full of praise, especially about the performances of the reporter's own countrymen, or full of severe criticism, particularly of the dangerous opponents from other nations. In Tokyo, only one of the judges had to assess his own compatriots. He was straightforward and unbiased, for he placed them seventh, tenth, and twentieth in a field of twenty-two riders from nine nations. A judge should not be expected to rate the riders of his own country with extreme severity in order to prove his impartiality. However, the correctness of this particular judge's opinion was confirmed by the verdicts of the other members of the jury.

To the Games in Mexico City in October 1968, eighteen nations delegated one hundred and twenty riders: Argentina, Australia, Belgium, Brazil, Canada, Chile, Democratic Republic of Germany, Federal Republic of Germany, France, Great Britain, Ireland, Italy, Japan, Mexico, Poland, Switzerland, the U.S.A., and the U.S.S.R.

Nine nations (Canada, Chile, Democratic Republic of Germany, Federal Republic of Germany, Great Britain, Mexico, Switzerland, the U.S.A., and the U.S.S.R.) with eight teams of three riders and two individual riders, that is, twenty-six riders, participated in the Grand Prix de Dressage. The individual medals were won by:

1. Kisimov (U.S.S.R.) on Ikhor
2. Neckermann (F.R.G.) on Mariano
3. Klimke (F.R.G.) on Dux

The team medals went to 1. F.R.G., 2. U.S.S.R., 3. Switzerland.

The Three-Day Event was contested by thirteen nations with forty-nine riders. The following teams won: 1. Great Britain, 2. U.S.A., 3. Australia.

Fifteen nations with forty-five riders competed in the Prix des Nations. The medals were awarded to the teams of: 1. Canada, 2. France, 3. F.R.G.

The test of the Grand Prix had undergone few changes and consisted of the principal test with thirty-three groups of exercises and the ride-off with twenty-three groups of exercises, as well as the four Collective Marks at the end of each test. Immediately after the principal test the winning teams were determined and the medals awarded.

The best 25 per cent of the participants of the principal test was summoned for a ride-off two days later. The sum of the scores of both tests decided the winner of the individual medals. The jury consisted of three judges placed on the short side of the arena opposite the rider's entrance and of one side judge. After completion of each ride all judges assembled at the stand of the president of the jury and compared their scores. Any considerable divergencies were corrected. All four judges together then decided the four Collective Marks which since 1960 have been part of the scores. Only one of the judges was to judge his fellow countrymen, whom he placed eighteenth, twentieth, and twenty-first.

There was extraordinary interest in the Grand Prix de Dressage as evidenced by the crowded grandstands. Unfortunately, the comparison of scores and the determination of the Collective Marks for which the judges met together after each ride took at least as much time as the presentation of the test itself—sometimes as long as half an hour. No wonder that the initially enthusiastic public lost the over-all view since it became impossible to compare the actual presentation of a rider with the final result of his scores. Consequently, the grandstands emptied rather rapidly, as had happened in Rome. When it became known that some of the judges had to correct up to seventeen (!) marks out of thirty-three in the test sheets of one and the same rider, the criticism of the judging system heightened in equestrian circles and also in the hippological press in most countries. I myself had the opportunity to see the three test sheets of one rider. One judge had corrected seven of his marks by adding one or two; another judge by deducting one to three. With such incidents it is certainly not possible to speak about a uniform conception which in fact should be expected in a jury elected by the FEI and subordinate to its regulations. Such abuses did not fail to arouse the FEI, and there were numerous attempts to remedy the system of judging by introducing various changes, which, however, did not always meet expectations. This is the subject of the following chapter which deals with the Olympic Games in Munich.

# 7

# Grand Prix de Dressage in Munich, 1972

Twenty-six nations (Argentina, Australia, Austria, Belgium, Bolivia, Brazil, Bulgaria, Canada, Chile, Denmark, Democratic Republic of Germany, Federal Republic of Germany, France, Great Britain, Hungary, Ireland, Italy, Japan, Mexico, Netherlands, Poland, Spain, Sweden, Switzerland, the U.S.A., and the U.S.S.R.) delegated one hundred and eighty riders to the equestrian events of the 20th Olympiad held from August 26 to September 11, 1972, in Munich.

Thirteen nations (Brazil, Canada, Denmark, Democratic Republic of Germany, Federal Republic of Germany, France, Great Britain, Japan, Netherlands, Sweden, Switzerland, the U.S.A., and the U.S.S.R.), with ten teams of three riders and three individual riders, competed in the Grand Prix de Dressage. The individual medals were won by:

1. Liselott Linsenhoff (F.R.G.) on Piaff
2. Elena Petuschkowa (U.S.S.R.) on Pepel

3. Josef Neckermann (F.R.G.) on Venetia

The team medals were awarded to 1. U.S.S.R., 2. F.R.G., 3. Sweden.

The Three-Day Event was entered by eighteen nations with seventy-three riders. The team medals went to: 1. Great Britain, 2. U.S.A., 3. F.R.G. Seventeen nations with sixty-six riders participated in the Prix des Nations (stadium jumping). The following teams won: 1. F.R.G., 2. U.S.A., 3. Italy.

Many readers will remember the Grand Prix de Dressage. Therefore it will be discussed in greater detail than that of the previous Games. Again it consisted of a principal test and a ride-off. In the principal test the winners of the team medals were determined and the better third of the participants qualified for the ride-off. The time allowed for the principal test was ten minutes. Thirty-eight groups of exercises were to be scored, and four Collective Marks were to be awarded after each rider had finished his presentation. The marks according to the regulations of the FEI were from ten to zero and corresponded to the scale given in the previous chapter.

The ride-off included twenty-four groups of exercises and the same four Collective Marks as in the principal test. The time allowed was seven minutes. The coefficient 2 was employed to multiply the marks for both pirouettes at the canter and the four Collective Marks, that is, there were altogether six coefficients of equal value.

Following is the entire Grand Prix test as it appeared on the test sheet, together with the scale of marks and the regulations for penal points. Also given is the test of the ride-off as printed on the test sheet, plus a sketch of the dressage arena complete with the measurements.

# GRAND PRIX de DRESSAGE
## (Principal Test)

**TIME ALLOWED: 10 MINUTES**

| | | TEST | DIRECTIVE IDEAS | Marks | Coefficient |
|---|---|---|---|---|---|
| 1 | A<br>X | Enter at collected canter<br>Halt - Immobility — Salute<br>Proceed at collected trot | The entry.<br>The halt and the transition from the halt. | 10 | |
| 2 | C<br>MXK<br>KA | Track to the right<br>Change rein at extended trot<br>Ordinary trot | The extension<br>The transitions. | 10 | |
| 3 | A<br>FXH | Ordinary canter<br>Change rein with change of leg at X | The extension, the calmness, and the change of leg. | 10 | |
| 4 | MXK<br>K | Change rein with change of leg at X<br>Collected canter | The extension, the calmness, the change of leg, and the transition. | 10 | |
| 5 | A<br>FXH<br>H | Collected trot<br>Change rein at extended trot<br>Ordinary trot | The extension.<br>The transitions. | 10 | |
| 6 | HCMBX | Ordinary trot | The extension. The balance. | 10 | |
| 7 | X<br><br><br><br>E | Halt - rein back 4 steps<br>advance 4 steps<br>rein back 6 steps<br>Immediately proceed at ordinary trot<br>Track to the left | The halt, the 2 rein-backs, the advance, and the connection between these movements. | 10 | |
| 8 | | The transitions from the ordinary trot to the halt and from the rein-back to the ordinary trot | | 10 | |
| 9 | XEKA<br>A | Ordinary<br>Collected trot | The extension. The balance.<br>The transition. | 10 | |
| 10 | FE | On two tracks | The correctness and the regularity.<br>The bearing and the flexion of the horse.<br>The balance. | 10 | |
| 11 | EM | On two tracks | The correctness and the regularity.<br>The bearing and the flexion of the horse.<br>The balance. | 10 | |
| 12 | MCH | Collected walk | The collection. The regularity. | 10 | |

| | | TEST | DIRECTIVE IDEAS | Marks | Coefficient |
|---|---|---|---|---|---|
| 13 | HXF<br>FAK | Change rein at extended walk<br>Ordinary walk | The extension.<br>The transition. | 10 | X2 |
| 14 | K<br>V<br>Between<br>L and P | Collected walk<br>Turn to the right<br><br>Half pirouette to the right | The regularity<br>of the half pirouette. | 10 | |
| 15 | Between<br>L and V | Half pirouette to the left | The regularity<br>of the half pirouette. | 10 | |
| 16 | | The collected walk KV (P) (V) L | The collection. The regularity. | 10 | |
| 17 | LPBX | First passage | The cadence. The regularity. | 10 | |
| 18 | X | First piaffe 10 to 12 steps | The cadence. The regularity. | 10 | |
| | | | Subtotal | 190 | |
| 19 | X | Proceed in passage. The transitions<br>from the passage to the piaffe and<br>from the piaffe to the passage | | 10 | |
| 20 | XESI | Second passage | The cadence. The regularity. | 10 | |
| 21 | I | Second piaffe 10 to 12 steps | The cadence. The regularity. | 10 | |
| 22 | I | Proceed in passage. The transitions<br>from the passage to the piaffe<br>and from the piaffe to the<br>passage | | 10 | |
| 23 | IRMG | Third passage | The cadence. The regularity. | 10 | |
| 24 | G<br>H | Proceed at collected canter left<br>Track to the left | The straightness and the calmness<br>of the transition from the<br>passage. | 10 | |
| 25 | HK<br>K | Extended canter<br>Collected canter | The extension. The straightness.<br>The transition. | 10 | |

| | | TEST | DIRECTIVE IDEAS | Marks | Coefficient |
|---|---|---|---|---|---|
| **26** | A | Down center line - 5 counter-changes of hand on two tracks to either side of the center line with change of leg at each change of direction. The first on two tracks to the left and the last to the right are of 3 strides, the 4 others of 6 strides | The correctness and the regularity of the 6 on two tracks and the 5 counter-changes. The bearing and the flexion of the horse. The balance. | 10 | |
| | G | Finishing on the right leg | | | |
| **27** | C | Track to the right | The extension. The collection. | 10 | |
| | MXK | Change rein at extended canter | The transitions and the change | | |
| | K | Collected canter and change of leg | of leg. | | |
| **28** | A | Down center line | The regularity of the pirouette. | 10 | X2 |
| | L | Pirouette to the left | | | |
| **29** | X | Change of leg | The regularity of the pirouette. | 10 | X2 |
| | I | Pirouette to the right | | | |
| **30** | C | Track to the right | | | |
| | MXK | On the diagonal, 9 changes of leg every second stride (finishing on the left leg) | The correctness and the straightness of the changes. | 10 | |
| **31** | FXH | On the diagonal, 15 changes of leg every stride (finishing on the right leg) | The correctness and the straightness of the changes. | 10 | |
| **32** | MF | Ordinary canter | The extension. The balance. The | 10 | |
| | F | Collected canter | straightness. The transition. | | |
| **33** | A | Down center line | The halt. | 10 | |
| | L | Halt - Rein back 4 steps - Immediately proceed at the fourth passage. | The rein-back. | | |
| **34** | | The transitions from the collected canter to the halt and from the rein-back to the passage | | 10 | |

| | TEST | DIRECTIVE IDEAS | Marks | Coefficient |
|---|---|---|---|---|
| 35 X | Circle to the right 8 meters diameter followed by the same circle to the left | The regularity of the two circles. The cadence and the regularity of the passage. The flexion of the horse. | 10 | |
| | | Subtotal | 380 | |
| 36 I | Third piaffe 10 to 12 steps | The cadence. The regularity. | 10 | |
| 37 I | Proceed in passage. The transitions from the passage to the piaffe and from the piaffe to the passage | | 10 | |
| 38 G | Halt - Immobility - Salute | The halt. The immobility. | 10 | |
| | Leave arena at a walk, on a long rein. | Total | 410 | |

| | Collective marks | Marks | Coefficient |
|---|---|---|---|
| **SCALE OF MARKS** | 1. Paces (freedom and regularity) | 10 | X2 |
| 10 excellent | 2. Impulsion (desire to move forward, elasticity of the steps, suppleness of the back, and engagement of the hind quarters) | 10 | X2 |
| 9 very good | | | |
| 8 good | 3. Submission (attention and confidence; harmony, lightness and ease of the movements; acceptance of the bridle and lightness of the forehand) | | |
| 7 fairly good | | 10 | X3 |
| 6 satisfactory | 4. Position, seat of the rider, correct use of the aids | 10 | X2 |
| 5 sufficient | To be deducted          Total | 500 | |
| 4 insufficient | | | |
| 3 fairly bad | — For every commenced second exceeding the time allowed: 1/2 mark | | |
| 2 bad | — Errors of the course and omissions are penalised | | |
| 1 very bad | 1st time = 2 marks | | |
| 0 not performed | 2nd time = 4 marks | | |
| | 3rd time = 8 marks | | |
| | 4th time = Elimination | | |
| | Total | | |

# RIDE-OFF TEST
## TIME ALLOWED: 7 MINUTES

| | | TEST | DIRECTIVE IDEAS | Marks | Coefficient |
|---|---|---|---|---|---|
| **1** | A<br>X | Enter at collected canter<br>Halt - Immobility - Salute - Proceed<br>at collected trot | The entry. The halt and the<br>transition from the halt. | 10 | |
| **2** | C<br>HXF<br>F | Track to the left<br>Change rein at extended trot<br>Collected trot | The extension,<br>The transitions, | 10 | |
| **3** | VXR | On two tracks | The regularity.<br>The bearing and the flexion of<br>the horse.<br>The balance. | 10 | |
| **4** | CHS<br>SEV<br>VKA<br>A | Extended trot<br>Collected trot<br>Extended trot<br>Collected trot | The extension. The collection.<br>The transitions. | 10 | |
| **5** | PXS | On two tracks | The regularity.<br>The bearing and the flexion of<br>the horse.<br>The balance. | 10 | |
| **6** | H<br>HCMG | Collected walk<br>Collected walk | The collection.<br>The regularity. | 10 | |
| **7** | G | First piaffe 10–12 steps | The cadence. The regularity. | 10 | |
| **8** | GHSI<br>RBX | First passage | The cadence.<br>The regularity. | 10 | |
| **9** | | The transitions from the collected<br>walk to the piaffe and from the<br>piaffe to the passage | | 10 | |
| **10** | X | Second piaffe 10–12 steps | The cadence. The regularity. | 10 | |
| **11** | XEVL<br>PFA | Second passage | The cadence.<br>The regularity. | 10 | |
| **12** | | The transitions from the passage to<br>the piaffe and from the piaffe<br>to the passage | | 10 | |

| | | TEST | DIRECTIVE IDEAS | Marks | Coefficient |
|---|---|---|---|---|---|
| 13 | A<br>KXM<br>M | Extended trot<br>Change rein at extended trot<br>Collected trot | The extension.<br>The transitions. | 10 | |
| 14 | C<br>HXF<br>F | Ordinary walk<br>Change rein at extended walk<br>Collected walk | The extension.<br>The transitions. | 10 | |
| 15 | A<br>KXM | Proceed at collected canter right<br>On the diagonal, 9 changes of leg<br>every 2nd stride (finishing on<br>the left leg) | The correctness and the<br>straightness of the changes. | 10 | |
| 16 | HXF | On the diagonal, 15 changes of leg<br>every stride (finishing on the<br>right leg) | The correctness and the straight-<br>ness of the changes. | 10 | |
| 17 | A<br>D | Down center line<br>Pirouette to the right | The regularity of the pirouette. | 10 | X2 |
| 18 | Between<br>D and G | 9 changes of leg every stride<br>(finishing on the left leg) | The correctness and the straight-<br>ness of the changes. | 10 | |
| 19 | G<br>C | Pirouette to the left<br>Track to the left | The regularity of the pirouette. | 10 | X2 |
| | | | Subtotal | 210 | |
| 20 | HK<br>K<br>A | Extended canter<br>Collected canter<br>Down center line | The extension. The straightness.<br>The transition. | 10 | |
| 21 | D<br>L | Collected trot<br>Third passage, advance to G | The cadence.<br>The regularity. | 10 | |
| 22 | G | Third piaffe 10 to 12 steps | The cadence. The regularity. | 10 | |
| 23 | | The transition from the passage to<br>the piaffe | | 10 | |
| 24 | G | After the piaffe, halt, immobility,<br>salute | The halt. The immobility. | 10 | |
| | | Leave arena at a walk, on a long rein. | Total | 260 | |

| TEST | DIRECTIVE IDEAS | Marks | Coefficient |
|---|---|---|---|
| | **Collective marks** | | |
| 1. | Paces (freedom and regularity) | 10 | X2 |
| 2. | Impulsion (desire to move forward, elasticity of the steps, suppleness of the back, and engagement of the hinds quarters) | 10 | X2 |
| 3. | Submission (attention and confidence; harmony, lightness, and ease of of the movements; acceptance of the bridle and lightness of the forehand) | 10 | X2 |
| 4. | Position, seat of the rider, correct use of the aids | 10 | X2 |
| | To be deducted                    Total | 340 | |

**SCALE OF MARKS**

10 excellent
9 very good
8 good
7 fairly good
6 satisfactory
5 sufficient
4 insufficient
3 fairly bad
2 bad
1 very bad
0 not performed

— For every commenced second exceeding the time allowed: 1/2 mark _____

— Errors of the course and omissions are penalised _____

1st time = 2 marks _____

2nd time = 4 marks _____

3rd time = 8 marks _____

4th time = Elimination _____

Total [        ]

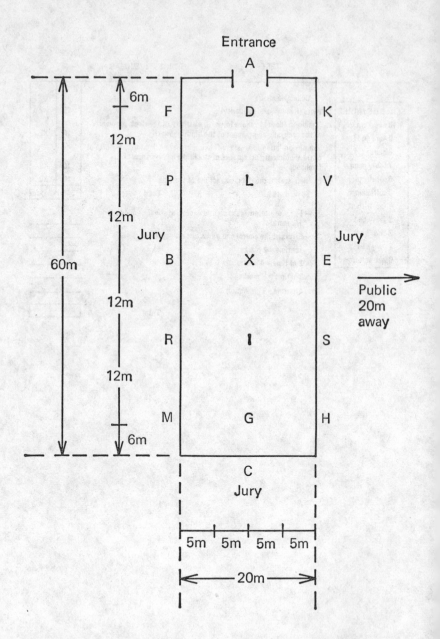

Here is my opinion about the two Olympic dressage tests. In a dressage test the rider should be given the opportunity to display his and his horse's abilities. For the judge it is important to gain a clear picture of what is presented in the test. He should form his opinion and find out the reason for faults that occur during the ride. Furthermore, the programme of a test should be laid out with beauty and harmony and correspond to the principles of classical horsemanship.

The author or authors of the principal test satisfactorily met the requirements and did justice to the concept of classical equitation. The beginning of the test distinguished itself by a logical structure offering the rider a chance to present the pure paces of his horse with distinct differences of tempo or speed as the horse moved straight forward with impulsion. Impulsion and suppleness in the collected paces present a beautiful sight in which riding approaches the realm of art. Frequent changes of tempo are the best way to achieve the gymnastic training of the horse and at the same time give proof of exactly that gymnastic schooling. Significantly, one of only three coefficients is attributed to the extended walk, and the walk in the different speeds is to be scored three times. This gives proof of concept and system in the construction of this test, for the walk more than the other paces reveals the correctness of training.

After the harmonious structure of the beginning the observer is disappointed by the way the two half pirouettes at the walk are laid out. These exercises are not well presented. When the distances for the turn is deducted there remains a stretch of not more than sixteen meters for the two of them. Besides, it seems illogical to award to these short exercises alone three of the total of thirty-eight marks.

The sport of dressage advocates the classical principles of horsemanship, which proclaim the preservation of the horse's natural movements. From this point of view the lay-out of the passage is incomprehensible. For three passages interrupted by two piaffes the rider has a distance of ninety-six meters complicated by six turns of ninety degrees. Here dressage perilously approaches circus riding. The passage, which in nature derives from a not fully released urge to go forward, consequently becomes an unaesthetic movement full of tenseness. This was clearly seen with most riders and stands in gross contrast to the promising beginning of the test. The extended canter, on the other hand, is very logically required before the two pirouettes on the center line. Here the rider has a chance to produce sufficient impulsion in his horse to guarantee the performance of an elastic, rhythmic pirouette.

The observer misses the exercises of riding with the reins in one hand and of giving the reins completely, preferably at the canter. These would contribute considerably to rounding off the over-all evaluation of horse and rider, as they are visible proof of absolute balance and of full harmony between the creatures. Furthermore, they would underline that the sport of competitive dressage naturally develops from basic general horsemanship and must never be anything like circus riding.

By means of the ride-off the individual medalists were selected among those competitors who qualified for it in the principal test. Since the scores of the principal test no longer count for the final evaluation, it is necessary and correct to demand again, in a different routine, the exercises that best reveal the basic training of the horse. In this respect the beginning of the ride-off is logically constructed. With a great variety of work at the trot the rider is offered a good opportunity to present his horse's impulsion and perfect balance, especially when riding through the corners of the arena at the extended trot. Changes of tempo rapidly alternating in short distances are the criterion for a sound foundation of schooling to be expected in a dressage horse of Olympic standard. I regret to say that in this exercise most riders displayed the horse's inability to produce a true extended trot immediately followed by a vivid and supple collected one—the fortissimo and the pianissimo of riding. Without consulting the programme of the test it was often difficult for the observer to find out what the rider was trying to perform. The brilliance of this exercise was too often lost in the indistinguishable uniform tempo in which it was presented. The periods of passage and piaffe were again to be ridden in the same unattractive bends and turns which had already interfered with the smooth continuation of movement in the principal test.

In both tests the harmonious flow of the different movements was encumbered by all sorts of kinks and curls, just as the rapid sequence of some exercises confused certain riders and hampered their performance. Consequently, watching thirty-three riders going through the test sometimes became tedious for even the most interested observer. This may be the explanation for the spontaneous applause with which the public received the British dressage rider Mrs. Lorna Johnstone on El Farruco. It was certainly prompted less by respect for the old lady than by the pleasure and relief after hours of watching the test to see at last a rider demonstrate distinct changes of speed and sportsmanlike impulsion.

The jury consisted of five judges who were strictly separated from each other. They had to form their opinions in total seclusion and dictate their evaluations, along with short remarks, if necessary, to their secretaries. After each ride the completed test sheets were taken to the scoring office. In the shortest possible time the results were evaluated and listed on the score board for everyone to see. The course of the Grand Prix unwound swiftly and the schedule was generally observed, which was a pleasant contrast to the endless conferences between the rides at the Grand Prix in Mexico in 1968.

The members of the jury were presided over by Colonel Nyblaeus (Sweden) here named Judge C, who was seated at the center of the short side. General de Breuil (France), on the short side at the president's left, is named Judge M. Mr. Herrera (Mexico) on the short side at the president's right is Judge H. Colonel Pollay (F.R.G.), at the center of the long side to the left, is Judge E. Mr. Pot (Netherlands), at the center of the long side to the left, is Judge B.

In the principal test the judges classified riders of their own nation as follows (the final placing is given in parentheses):

| Judge C (Sweden) | Hakansson | 331 marks on place 2 | (5) |
|---|---|---|---|
| | Swaab | 316 marks on place 7 | (7) |
| | von Rosen | 313 marks on place 9 | (11) |
| Judge M (France) | Le Rolland | 306 marks on place 20 | (23) |
| Judge E (F.R.G.) | Linsenhoff | 368 marks on place 1 | (1) |
| | Neckermann | 350 marks on place 2 | (3) |
| | Schlüter | 319 marks on place 9 | (9) |
| Judge B (Netherlands) | van Doorne | 305 marks on place 17 | (18) |
| | Benedictus | 301 marks on place 21 | (27) |
| | Swaab | 210 marks on place 27 | (28) |

In the ride-off the judges scored:

| | | | | | |
|---|---|---|---|---|---|
| Judge C (Sweden) | Hakansson | 226 | marks on place | 2 | (6) |
| | von Rosen | 215 | marks on place | 6 | (8) |
| | Swaab | 210 | marks on place | 8 | (10) |
| Judge E (F.R.G.) | Linsenhoff | 254 | marks on place | 1 | (1) |
| | Neckermann | 247 | marks on place | 2 | (3) |
| | Schlüter | 233 | marks on place | 3 | (7) |

The observations made by an expert seated in the grandstands may help to form an over-all opinion of the performances as well as of the evaluations of the various judges. It is then left to the competitor and the attentive observer to compare my notes with the official results. It goes without saying that some exercises may be better observed from the judge's platforms than from the grandstands. On the other hand, it should be remembered that sometimes the interested observer may watch more attentively and see more of what goes on than the judge, who, besides following the rider's activities, must also concentrate on his scores.

During the performances I recorded my observations and opinions on tape. These records, which are presented here, have not been edited, because the aim is to conserve the originality and freshness of the observations. The evaluations are based on the regulations of the Fédération Equestre Internationale, which, after all, are obligatory for rider and judge as well. As the guideline for my observations I have taken the main items in the Rules on Dressage:

1. Purity of the paces, freedom and regularity of the movement.
2. Harmony, lightness in all movements which conveys the impression of complete confidence, the rider riding with invisible and inaudible aids. Apparently the rider thinks and the horse executes his thoughts.

3. Adequate engagement of the hind quarters which evenly distributes the weight of horse and rider and lightens the forehand, the horse carrying himself and taking a light and steady contact on the bit.

4. Absolute straightness of the horse on straight lines as well as in turns and circles. The hind legs must step forward in the direction of the hoof prints of the forefeet.

5. The walk should be pure, with rhythmic and regular steps and with unconstrained position of head and neck. The trot must be regular and supple with active hind quarters, the rider seemingly part of the horse. The change of tempo, especially, should come about with ease and grace upon the rider's command. At the collected tempo the cadenced steps should remain lively, supple, and in regular rhythm. The rider should be able to immediately send his horse forward in an extended trot and collect him again without difficulty in supple and easy transitions. The canter must be a pure three-beat pace which when changing tempo differs in the ground gained to the front but not in the rhythm of the bounds. This is possible only with sufficient activity of the hind quarters.

6. In the steady and light contact with the bit—in movement as well as in the rein-back or at the standstill— the horse's concentration upon his rider becomes obvious as do his lightness and suppleness.

In my record of the principal test I have listed the riders by nationality and in the order in which they started. This coverage does not pretend to give a minute description of the complete program of the test nor of each ride but is meant to point out the strong and weak moments which became obvious in the course of the test.

## PRINCIPAL TEST

*Switzerland*

Hermann Dür on Sod. No immobility at the halt and salute. Trot is not begun directly from the halt, extended trot does not gain sufficient ground; in extension the horse takes a longer stride with the forelegs than with the hind legs and consequently has to withdraw the front leg before touching the ground. He becomes crooked at the strike-off, does not go sufficiently forward at the medium canter. Transition into the collected trot is not fluent. Second extended trot is somewhat better but with uneven steps towards the end of the diagonal. Crooked halt at X. Alternated rein-back and going forward is not supple enough and not performed with the prescribed number of steps. Half pass to the left with incorrect position of head and neck, somewhat better to the right. Uneven steps in the collected walk. The tempo is not maintained in the extended walk, which does not gain ground to the front. A slight disturbance before the half pirouette at the walk to the right. The half pirouette to the left is performed with incorrect position of head. The passage is merely outlined. Slight disorder before the piaffe. Piaffe only outlined; the horse does not have his hocks under him. Second piaffe is somewhat better in rhythm but again with the hind legs not stepping sufficiently under the body. The collected canter is crooked; the zigzag at the canter is well performed. The extended canter covers sufficient ground but deviates from the diagonal. Pirouette to the left is well performed; in the pirouette to the right the rhythm of the canter is lost. In the flying changes after two strides the horse throws his hind quarters to the side. One fault in the flying changes at every stride. Good extended canter, good halt. Rein-back with resistance. Last passage is hasty and without brilliance. Uneven steps in the last piaffe. The horse does not stand still at the final halt.

Judge C: 301 (16), H: 271 (29), M: 299 (25), E: 298 (19), B: 297 (25), Total: 1466 (114).*

Christine Stückelberger on Granat. The hind legs do not step under the body of the horse at the halt. The trot is not begun from the halt. Too much position to the right in the extended trot. Slightly crooked at the strike-off. Medium canter does not gain sufficient ground; in the change of leg the hind legs do not take a full stride. In the second change over the diagonal at the canter the horse loses the direction. Crooked canter left before the transition into the collected trot. Extended trot is regular and well gaining ground but there is no difference to the medium trot. Besides there is a slight disturbance in the medium trot. Rein-back comes crooked and with the hind legs spread. Transition into the trot is not begun immediately from the rein-back. The rider guides her horse with very unsteady hands. Uneven steps in half pass to the left; insufficient lateral position in that to the right. Steps of amble in the collected walk. Extended walk is hasty,

* In parentheses next to the individual marks there is the place mark of each judge and next to the total mark there is the sum of the place marks of all five judges.

14. Major Podhajsky on Nero—Bronze medal 1936
15. Captain Moser on Revue (Gold medal 1948 on Hummer)

16. Colonel Jousseaume on Harpagon—Silver medal 1948 and Bronze medal 1952

17. Captain Boltenstern on Krest (Bronze medal 1948 on Trumpf)

18. Mrs. Hartel on Jubilee—Silver medal 1952 and 1956

). Major St. Cyr on Juli—Gold medal
)56 (Gold medal 1952 on Master
ufus)

20. Mr. Filatow on Absent—Gold medal 1960 and Bronze medal 1964

with unsteady contact; it does not cover sufficient ground. In the half pirouette to the right the hind quarters remain inactive. There are uneven steps in the half pirouette to the left. First passage is good; uneven steps in the piaffe; the transitions, however, are good. In the second piaffe the rhythm is again lost. The horse is crooked at the extended canter. The transition into the collected canter is not very supple. There is too much position to the right in the zigzag half pass and not enough to the left. The extended canter does not gain sufficient ground. The pirouette to the left is good; in that to the right the rhythm is lost. One fault in the flying changes after two strides. Flying changes at every stride are good. The corners of the arena are inaccurately ridden; the horse sways and does not remain on the track along the long side. Good transition into the collected canter. At the halt the hind legs do not step under the body of the horse. Rein-back lacks suppleness and the transition into the passage does not follow immediately from the rein-back. The circles at the passage are not traced round but oval. The rider leans her upper part back and rides with a wagging head and very unsteady hands. The last piaffe and passage are well performed.

Judge C: 296 (18), H: 305 (10), M: 311 (15), E: 305 (16), B: 311 (14), Total: 1528 (73).

Maria Äschbacher on Charlamp. Good entry and halt. The horse begins to move at the walk instead of at the trot. Extended trot gains no ground and there is no difference to the medium trot. No forward urge at the medium canter; the horse throws his hind quarters to the side in the flying change. Stiff transition into the collected trot. Extended trot does not cover ground; there are uneven steps at X. The rider leans her upper part back and wags her head. The halt comes not from the trot but with intermediate steps of walk. Rein-back-forward-rein-back: the horse is behind the bit and does not take the number of steps prescribed. Medium trot without impulsion. Half pass to the left with little lateral position, the horse is twisting his tail. He is behind the bit in the half pass to the right. Collected walk is not collected enough; extended walk is better but with indistinct transitions into the medium and collected walk. In the half pirouette at the walk to the right little activity of the hind quarters; horse comes to a stop in the half pirouette to the left. First and second passages are weak and with uneven steps, halting transition into the piaffe, which is rather mediocre. Medium canter does not cover ground; no forward urge in the collected canter. Zigzag half pass not very supple, the horse comes behind the bit. Only a few bounds of extended canter, collected canter is in four-beat. In the pirouette to the left the rhythm of the canter is lost. Pirouette to the right is better but still with rather irregular rhythm. Flying changes at every second stride deviate from the diagonal. In the flying changes at every stride the horse's hind legs do not always take a full stride. In the medium canter the horse is behind the bit and without forward urge. Good halt. Passage on the circles sometimes with irregular strides and a very uneven tempo. Rider guides her horse with her hands widely separated. Judge C: 286 (20), H: 277 (26), M: 301 (23), E: 247 (32), B: 278 (29), Total: 1389 (130).

*U.S.S.R.*

Ivan Kisimov on Ikhor. Good entry and halt. The horse remains immobile and on the bit. The trot is well begun from the halt. Extended trot not fully satisfactory. Regular and lively medium canter. Very little difference to the collected canter. Extended trot again not fully satisfactory, and with too much action of the forelegs. No distinct difference to the medium trot. The rein-back is good. Half passes very fluent and precisely performed. Uneven steps in the transition to the collected walk. Extended walk not fully satisfactory. Second collected walk good. Not enough activity of the hind quarters in the two half pirouettes at the walk. First passage expressive. Piaffe and second passage good and with very beautiful transitions but with the horse agitating his tail. Distinct changes of tempo at the canter; very good zigzag half passes. The bounds of canter might have been more lively in the pirouette to the left. The rhythm of the canter is lost in the pirouette to the right. Very good flying changes at the canter at two and one strides. Distinct transition into the medium canter. Slight resistance at the beginning of the passage from the rein-back. Passage very brilliant. A very harmonious performance, however somewhat devalued by the fact that the horse swishes his tail. The rider often has the tread of his stirrup up against his heel and sticks his elbows out.

Judge C: 322 (6), H: 342 (5), M: 357 (2), E: 340 (3), B: 340 (5), Total: 1701 (21).

Iwan Kalita on Tarif. Very good entry and halt but the horse does not stand motionless. Very impulsive extended trot; however, the rider is bumped about in the saddle. Medium canter might show more impulsion; the tempo is evenly maintained. Supple transition into the collected trot and good transition into the extended trot. The change of tempo into the medium trot is not sufficiently distinct. Rein-back is supple; however, the number of steps is not observed. In the half passes the horse comes above the bit. Good transition into the walk, but in the collected walk the position of the horse's head is too free. Extended walk is regular and gains ground to the front with long strides. The rider hardly ever takes his horse precisely through the corners of the arena. The half pirouette at the walk to the right is very good; half pirouette to the left is good. Good transition into the passage, which is regular and expressive. Good transition into the piaffe, which is somewhat disturbed in rhythm. The same with the second piaffe. The performance of the passage throughout regular and beautiful. Good strike-off into the canter from the passage. Distinct difference of tempo at the canter. Very good half pass zigzags, good extended canter. The transition into the collected canter is performed without forward urge. Good pirouette to the left; the horse becomes crooked before the pirouette to the right, in which the rhythm is lost. Good flying changes at the canter at two and one time. Good transition into the medium and collected canter. Good halt, rein-back, and move-off into the passage. Very regular tempo in the passage on both circles. Good transition into the last piaffe, in which, however, the rhythm is lost. Good last halt.

Judge C: 326 (4), H: 336 (6), M: 338 (8), E: 325 (5), B: 322 (12), Total: 1647 (35).

Elena Petuschkowa on Pepel. Good entry, but the horse's hind quarters are not engaged at the halt. Extended trot is hasty and running with very little difference to the medium trot. Strike-off slightly crooked; medium canter is mediocre. Extended trot regular but gains insufficient ground. Good halt and supple rein-back-forward-rein-back. Half pass to the left is somewhat hesitant; half pass to the right is good. Good transition into the collected walk. Extended walk is hasty, does not cover sufficient ground. The changes of tempo at the walk are indistinct. During the transition into the collected walk there are some piaffe-like steps. Half pirouette to the right with little activity of the hind quarters. Half pirouette to the left is good. At the beginning of the first passage the horse becomes very crooked and agitates his tail. The passage in parts is full of impulsion. In the transition into the piaffe irregular steps which continue in the piaffe itself. The horse's tail is very agitated during the second passage. Extended canter is very good and with distinct difference to the collected canter. Very good half pass zigzags; excellent extended canter. Very good pirouette to the left, good pirouette to the right. Very good flying changes after two strides, in one of the flying changes at every stride the horse does not take a full stride. Very good medium canter and changes of tempo. Very good halt, rein-back, and move-off into the passage. The rhythm of the passage might be a little slower but the passage is very regular and expressive. In the last piaffe the horse again swishes his tail. Good position of the rider. Excellent walk on the loose rein when leaving the arena.

Judge C: 352 (1), H: 360 (2), M: 365 (1), E: 323 (7), B: 347 (2), Total: 1747 (13).

## Federal Republic of Germany

Liselott Linsenhoff on Piaff. Good entry and halt. The horse anticipates the move-off into the trot. Extended trot with irregular steps; crooked strike-off into the canter. Good medium canter. In the second flying change on the diagonal the horse throws his hind quarters to the side. He is crooked before the transition into the collected trot. Irregular steps in the second extended trot. The prescribed number of steps is not observed in the alternating rein-back and forward. The half pass to the left is not very supple and not performed on the prescribed line. That to the right is better. Extended trot is not fully satisfactory and does not cover sufficient ground to the front; there are hasty steps. Both half pirouettes at the walk are good. First passage is good; the horse steps back in the piaffe. Second piaffe is better. Collected canter is not very supple; half pass zigzags are good. In the pirouette to the left the rhythm is lost, the pirouette to the right fails completely. One fault in the flying changes at the canter both at two and at every stride. Good medium canter, transition into the collected canter is not very supple. The horse comes to a halt after intermediate steps at the walk; he moves off into the piaffe instead of the passage. Afterwards the passage is very regular; the rider, however, is bumped about in the saddle. Last halt is good.

Judge C: 326 (4), H: 367 (1), M: 343 (7), E: 368 (1), B: 359 (1), Total: 1763 (14).

Karin Schlüter on Liostro. Entry and halt are good; the horse moves off directly from the standstill. Very good extended trot and distinct transition to the medium trot. Strike-off into the canter is slightly crooked. Medium canter is regular and impulsive. Rider traces precisely the figures of the program. At times the horse is crooked at the canter on the left lead. At the extended trot the horse's head and neck are raised too much; his neck becomes short, hence no co-ordination of the action of his forelegs and hind quarters. Insufficient difference to the medium trot. Very good rein-back-forward-rein-back and transition into medium trot. Half pass to the left is fluent, there is a slight hesitation during the half pass to the right. Visible difference between medium and collected walk. Half pirouette to the right with inactive hind legs; half pirouette to the left is better. Good transition into the passage and piaffe, which, however, is disturbed in rhythm by the horse's resistance. Second piaffe fails also. Rider is constantly pulling her heels up and tugging at the reins. Extended canter on the left lead slightly crooked. Good half pass zigzags; extended canter on the diagonal might be more expressive. The rhythm of the canter is lost in the pirouette to the left. Pirouette to the right is even worse. Two faults in the flying changes at two strides. Crooked collected canter on the left lead. Flying changes at every stride again with faults, the horse kicking against the spur at the beginning of this exercise. Good transition into the medium canter and again into the collected one. Halt with the hind legs not engaged.

Judge C: 328 (3), H: 289 (16), M: 347 (4), E: 319 (9), B: 331 (8), Total: 1614 (40).

Josef Neckermann on Venetia. Good entry and halt, good move-off into the trot. Good extended trot and distinct transition into the medium trot. Crooked strike-off. Good medium canter; slight hesitation during the transition into the collected canter. The horse becomes crooked during the transition into the collected trot. Good extended trot but no difference to the medium trot. Rein-back-forward-rein-back are supple, but the prescribed number of steps is not observed. Transition from the medium into the collected trot is not very supple. Good half pass to the left. The horse stumbles and strikes off into the canter before the transition into the walk. The collected walk is a pure amble. The extended walk is good; again ambling steps in the medium and collected walk. Half pirouette to the right is good; half pirouette to the left is too large. Uneven steps in the first passage; the first steps of piaffe after the transition are also uneven. During the second piaffe the horse steps back. This passage is very good. Half pass zigzags are not very supple and sometimes hesitant. Extended and collected canters are very good. Good pirouette to the left. In the flying change the horse's hind legs do not make a full stride. Pirouette to the right is good. Flying changes at two strides are good; the horse becomes crooked at the collected canter on the left lead. Good flying changes at every stride. Medium and collected canters are good. Passage after the rein-back begins with uneven steps. Both circles are performed with irregularity, oval shaped and at an uneven tempo. Last piaffe is good; in the transition into the fifth passage the horse comes above the bit.

Judge C: 314 (8), H: 355 (4), M: 347 (4), E: 350 (2), B: 340 (5), Total: 1706 (23).

## Sweden

Ulla Hakansson on Ajax. Halt with the hind legs not engaged. Extended trot is regular and covers much ground. Crooked strike-off. Medium canter is regular and full of impulsion. Horse becomes crooked during the transition into the collected trot. Very good extended trot. The rider does not sit deep enough in the saddle. Very good and supple rein-back-forward-rein-back. Good transition into the medium trot. Half pass to the left is not supple enough; the horse has too much position to the right in the half pass to the right. The horse is not sufficiently collected in the collected walk, does not cover enough ground to the front in the extended walk; there are hasty steps. Both half pirouettes are good. First passage is somewhat hasty at the beginning. Very good transition into the piaffe. First piaffe is good. Second passage and piaffe are very good. The most expressive piaffe and passage presented so far.* Transition into the collected canter is not a forward movement. Pirouettes to the left and right very good. Flying changes at every second stride are very good and going well forward. Medium canter covers insufficient ground. Good halt and rein-back but no immediate transition from the rein-back into the passage. Fourth passage good at the beginning, then with uneven, steps on both circles. Transition and third piaffe are good. Very good final halt. Pleasant position of the rider and excellent use of the aids.

Judge C; 331 (2), H: 357 (3), M: 311 (15), E: 321 (8), B: 329 (9), Total: 1649 (37).

Ninna Swaab on Casanova. Good entry and halt. Move-off at the trot directly from the halt. Very impulsive extended trot and distinct transition into the medium trot. Horse becomes slightly crooked at the strike-off. Medium canter full of impulsion and with a good flying change at X. Very distinct transition into the collected canter. Extended trot does not cover sufficient ground to the front; consequently there is little difference to the medium trot. Halt and rein-back-forward-rein-back are good. Horse becomes crooked in the transition from the medium to the

---

* This mark refers to those competitors seen in the course of the test up to this moment, that is, the first riders of each national team discussed so far.

collected trot on the short side of the arena. Half pass to the left lacking impulsion; half pass to the right with insufficient lateral position. Good transition into the walk. Collected walk lacks in collection; extended walk is good, distinct transition to the medium walk. Rider does not take the horse correctly through the corners of the arena. There is a hesitation during the transition into the collected walk. Half pirouette to the right with little activity of the hind legs. Hesitant transition into the first passage; the passage itself is quite good. Piaffe and transition into the second passage rather mediocre, which may also be said about the second piaffe, in which the horse tends to step back. Slightly crooked at the canter on the left lead. Half pass zigzag is good; very good transition into the extended canter. The rhythm of the canter is lost in the pirouette to the left. The pirouette to the right is quite good. Flying changes at two strides are good; the line of the diagonal is precisely observed. Good flying changes at every stride, but the horse agitates his tail. Good transitions into the medium and collected canter. Halt and rein-back are good, but no immediate transition into the fourth passage. Brilliant passage on the circles. Uneven transition into the last piaffe. Some very good strides in the last passage. Good final halt.

Judge C: 316 (7), H: 313 (9), M: 333 (9), E: 319 (9), B: 341 (4), Total: 1622 (38).

Maud von Rosen on Lucky Boy. Good entry and halt. Move-off into the trot immediately from the halt. Extended trot is good and covers ground to the front. Distinct transition to the medium trot. The horse does not go forward in the medium canter; he kicks against the spur, becomes crooked in the transition to the collected trot.

Again impulsive extended trot with gain of ground. Good halt at X. Rein-back-forward-rein-back with little suppleness; good transition into the medium trot. Half passes are not very fluent, to the left especially. Collected walk is insufficiently collected, extended walk hasty and without gain of ground. Uneven steps in the transition to the medium walk. At the collected walk the horse opens his mouth and pulls up his tongue. Half pirouette to the right without activity of the hind legs. The same in the pirouette to the left. Passage is too hasty; irregular transition into the piaffe, the horse steps back; he swishes his tail in the second piaffe. Good changes of tempo in the canter which follows. The rhythm of the canter is lost in the half pass zigzags, in which there is insufficient activity of the horse's hind quarters. Very good extended canter and transition into the collected one. In both pirouettes the rhythm of the canter is lost. Good flying changes at two strides and at every stride. Impulsive medium canter and good transition into the collected canter. Good halt and rein-back. The move-off into the passage from the rein-back is good. On the two circles the passage is hasty and in irregular tempo. There are uneven steps.

Judge C: 313 (9), H: 304 (12), M: 332 (10), E: 309 (13), B: 320 (13), Total: 1578 (57).

*Netherlands*

Friederica Benedictus on Turista. Good halt and move-off. No difference between extended and medium trot. Good medium canter. Rein-back-forward-rein-back are not very supple. Differences of tempo at the trot and canter hardly ever to be seen. Half pass to the left rather painstaking and not very supple, somewhat better to the right. Pace-like steps at the collected walk. The extended walk covers ground to the front but becomes hasty towards the end of the diagonal. Again pace-like steps at the collected walk. Half pirouettes with little suppleness. Passage and piaffe merely indicated; they are the weakest part of the performance. Half pass zigzags very irregular. Extended canter gains no ground. Pirouette to the left is good; pirouette to the right is too large. Faults in the flying changes at two strides; flying changes at every stride well forward. Rein-back very painstaking and not supple. Passage merely indicated; last piaffe again fails. The rider's position is not very supple. She bumps about in the saddle.

Judge C: 278 (22), H: 266 (32), M: 295 (28), E: 280 (26), B: 301 (21), Total: 1420 (129).

Annie van Doorne on Pericles. Abrupt halt. The horse does not move off from the halt. Extended trot does not cover ground; the horse swishes his tail. Again agitated tail in the strike-off into the canter. Medium canter without forward urge and with again agitated tail. No suppleness but irregular steps at the transition into the collected trot. Extended trot does not gain ground. The horse is tense. No noticeable difference to the medium trot. Rein-back-forward-rein-back are good. Half pass to the left very tense and with a swishing tail. The movement to the right is better, but the horse's tail is very agitated. Good transition into the collected walk. The extended walk is hasty and does not gain ground. The horse becomes too short in his neck. No difference between medium and collected walk. Both half pirouettes are good. The passage without brilliance and with little activity of the hind quarters. Hesitant transition into the piaffe. Irregular steps in the piaffe. The same in the second passage and piaffe. The contact with the bit is too strong; the horse lies too much on the rein. No noticeable differences of tempo at the canter. Half pass zigzags quite good; no gain of ground in the extended canter. Both pirouettes are good. In the flying changes at two strides the horse throws his hind quarters to the side and swishes his tail. The same is to be said about the flying changes at every stride. In these exercises the rider's aids are very visible. At the halt the horse is on his forehand. Good rein-back and good move-off into the passage. The passage itself, however, without brilliance. The circles at the passage are very irregular. Transition into the piaffe is not very supple. At the halt the horse does not step under his body with his hind legs. Performance of a tolerably obedient horse with little charm and suppleness.

Judge C: 274 (23), H: 289 (16), M: 311 (15), E: 301 (17), B: 305 (17), Total: 1480 (88).

John Swaab on Maharadscha. When entering the arena the horse shies and does not remain immobile at the halt. The move-off does not come from the halt. The extended trot does not gain ground; the rider bumps in the saddle. His hands are very unsteady. Crooked strike-off into the canter. The rider rides very imprecisely through the corners. No difference between medium and collected canter. Bad transition into the collected trot. The second extended trot is better than the first, but there is no difference to the medium trot. Slight resistance in the rein-back when alternately reining back and going forward. Hasty medium trot with running steps. In the half passes the horse sometimes adopts a wrong position. Collected walk is inadequately collected; the walk is hasty and does not gain ground. The rider rides on a loose rein instead of in contact with the bit. No activity of the hind legs in both half pirouettes. Passage is merely indicated; the piaffe fails. The horse's legs are riveted to the ground. Second piaffe is somewhat better but still not supple. Differences of tempo are noticeable at the canter. Half pass zigzags are very imprecise and vague. Pirouette to the left is good; the rhythm of the canter is lost in the pirouette to the right. Good flying changes at two strides but deviating from the diagonal. Many faults in the flying changes at every stride. The horse shows resistance. Distinct collected canter and transition. Good halt and rein-back. Fourth passage is too hasty and superficial. Halt not square.

Judge C: 260 (31), H: 273 (28), M: 300 (24), E: 281 (25), B: 295 (27), Total: 1409 (135).

*Great Britain*

Jennie Loriston-Clarke on Kadett. The first periods at the trot are good. The medium canter does not gain sufficient ground to the front. Very good transition from the canter into the collected trot. Extended trot precipitated and without gain of ground. There is hardly a difference to the medium trot. Resistance in the alternating rein-back and forward; there is a disturbance in the movement of the rein-back. Half pass to the left is fluent, but the horse adopts a wrong position of his head. Somewhat better to the right. No difference between collected and extended walk. The latter does not cover ground. Half pirouette to the right is good, that to the left is too large. Passage is superficial and without expression. Piaffe merely indicated. Uneven steps in the second passage and piaffe.

The horse strikes off into the canter in the third passage. The two airs of Haute Ecole cannot be counted as such. Half pass zigzags fluent and expressive. In the extended trot the action of the horse is somewhat running and hasty. The rhythm of the canter is lost in both pirouettes. Fault in the flying changes at every stride. Good position of the rider and good use of the aids in the flying changes. Good transitions into the medium and collected canter. Good halt. Passage and piaffe flat and with faults. Passage on the circles is better than on a straight line. Piaffe again insufficient. Good final halt.

Judge C: 270 (26), H: 292 (15), M: 298 (26), E: 291 (22), B: 299 (24), Total: 1450 (113).

Margret D. Lawrence on San Fernando. After the halt the horse is resistant and refuses to move on at the trot. Extended trot in great tension. Medium canter very impulsive and brilliant. Slight disorder at the flying change at X. Second diagonal is better. Extended trot again very tense and with uneven steps; there is no visible difference to the collected trot. The horse does not remain immobile at the halt. Resistance in the rein-back, which turns crooked. The whole exercise of alternating rein-back and forward fails. Uneven and tense steps during the transition into the medium trot. In the half pass to the left the horse is behind the bit and becomes irregular in the sequence of his steps. In the half pass to the right the horse resists the sideways movement and vigorously agitates his tail. Collected walk very irregular; short hasty steps in the extended walk, which does not gain ground. The period at the walk is practically not performed. Before the half pirouette some piaffe-like steps. The half pirouette to the right is much too large and deviating from the prescribed

line. The half pirouette to the left is better, but the horse
does not maintain the walk but anticipates the passage.
The first few steps of passage are good. The transition
into the piaffe and the piaffe itself are irregular, the horse
stepping back. The extended canter is inadequate; the
horse comes above the bit and becomes crooked. Half
pass zigzags may be called satisfactory. The extended
canter is performed in a few bounds only. Pirouette to the
left quite good, but the rider holds the horse too tightly
and does not dare to slacken the reins. In the pirouette to
the right the rhythm of the canter is lost. Flying changes
at two strides are performed without fault, but the rider
holds the horse much too tightly. Faults at the beginning
of the flying changes at every stride. The changes of
tempo at the canter are not performed because the rider
does not dare to let the horse go forward. Rein-back very
tense; the horse does not move off into the passage right
away. In the passage the tension of the horse increases
and causes uneven steps before the transition into the
piaffe. The final halt is good.

Judge C: 239 (33), H: 267 (31), M: 239 (33), E: 243
(33), B: 254 (33), Total: 1242 (163).

Hilda Lorna Johnstone on El Farruco. Halt with the hind
legs not engaged. Extended trot very impulsive. Good
transition into the medium canter. Good flying change.
Extended trot gaining well ground to the front; no visible
difference to the medium trot. Good halt; supple rein-
back-forward-rein-back. Good transition into the medium
trot. No transition into the collected trot, consequently
the two half passes fail. Collected walk is somewhat
hasty; the horse does not take distinct strides. Extended
walk is also hasty without lengthening of the stride.

Collected walk is good; both half pirouettes are too large and with insufficient activity of the hind legs. In the passage the horse does not lift his feet. The piaffe is irregular, the horse just trips about on the spot. Good extended canter with distinct transition into the collected canter. The prescribed number of bounds is not observed in the half pass zigzags. Good extended canter; both pirouettes are too large and lose the rhythm of the canter. Very good flying changes at two strides, excellent flying changes at every stride. Good medium canter which covers much ground to the front. Halt with the horse's hind legs not engaged. Passage irregular; piaffe is also bad.

Judge C: 307 (13), H: 307 (11), M: 349 (3), E: 313 (12), B: 300 (23), Total: 1576 (62).

## Democratic Republic of Germany

Horst Köhler on Imanuel. Entry at a four-beat canter. Halt with the hind legs not engaged. Extended trot and medium canter not brilliant; disorder at the flying change, the horse swishes his tail. Very hesitant transition into the collected trot. Insufficient extended trot, the horse's hind legs do not step sufficiently under his body. No difference to the medium trot. The rein-back-forward-rein-back is not supple and the number of steps is not observed. Half pass to the left is hesitant; in the half pass to the right the horse does not adopt sufficient lateral position. Extended walk is regular but might cover more ground to the front. The transition from the medium to the collected walk is not visible. Half pirouette to the right is very inactive, that to the left is insufficient. First passage with uneven steps. Irregular piaffe which is some kind of balancé. In the second piaffe the horse steps back.

Good half pass zigzags at the canter; extended canter lacks forward urge. The rhythm of the canter is lost in the pirouette to the left. In the flying changes at two strides the horse throws his hind quarters to the side. Faults in the flying changes at every stride. The horse swishes his tail. Distinct transition into the medium and collected canter. The halt comes after several steps at the walk. Uneven steps at the passage, the horse strikes off into the canter. The last piaffe is again irregular. Halt with the hind legs not engaged.

Judge C: 297 (17), H: 287 (20), M: 273 (31), E: 301 (17), B: 328 (10), Total: 1486 (95).

Wolfgang Müller on Semafor. Good halt, immediate move-off into the trot. Extended trot might cover more ground to the front. Good strike-off into the canter; medium canter lacks impulsion, consequently flat transition into the collected canter. Good transition into the trot and good extended trot. Not very visible difference to the medium trot. Rein-back is not very supple in the exercise of alternating rein-back and forward. The number of steps is not observed. The half pass to the left is not very supple; it is a rather abrupt movement; the rider bumps in the saddle. Inadequate lateral position in the half pass to the right; the horse does not reach the prescribed mark of the arena. Good transition into the walk; collected walk with insufficient collection. Extended walk gains well ground to the front. Distinct transitions into medium and collected walk. Both half pirouettes are good. Passage is brilliant with a good transition into the piaffe. Both times in the piaffe the horse does not come off the ground with his front legs. Passage again good. At the strike-off the horse becomes violent and tries to rush off. Half pass zigzags rather irregular. Distinct transition into the extended canter, which, however, comes to an end at X instead of at K. Left pirouette is good; in the pirouette to the right the activity of the hind legs dies down. Good flying changes at two strides; however, the horse deviates from the diagonal. Flying changes at every stride fail because of severe faults at the beginning of the exercise. Good medium and collected canter. Halt with the hind legs not under the horse. Good move-off into the passage after the rein-back. The passage on both circles is good. Towards the end of the performance the passage steadily improves. Good transition into the piaffe, again the horse's front legs do not come off the ground. Final halt with the hind legs not engaged.

Judge C: 308 (12), H: 284 (21), M: 315 (12), E: 306 (14), B: 308 (15), Total: 1521 (74).

*United States of America*

Edith Master on Dahlwitz. The horse does not remain immobile at the halt. Extended trot gains ground to the front. Crooked strike-off; medium canter lacks forward urge. Rider jerks her upper part back and forward. No difference between medium and collected canter. The extended trot does cover ground, but the hind quarters of the horse are not sufficiently active. No difference to the medium trot. Not enough suppleness in the alternating rein-back and forward. Crooked in the collected trot on the short side of the arena. Half pass to the left with insufficient lateral flexion, somewhat better to the right. Extended walk is hasty and does not gain ground to the front. Half pirouette to the right is too large, that to the left is better. Passage is merely indicated; no activity of the hind quarters, consequently there is a bad transition into the piaffe, which again is merely indicated. Second passage and piaffe are somewhat better. Good strike-off into the canter from the passage. Half pass zigzags are sufficient. Extended canter does not cover sufficient ground. Both pirouettes are good. Flying changes at two strides lack impulsion and are executed with short bounds. Use of the aids is very visible. Faults in the flying changes at every stride which lack forward urge. Rider gives very visible rein aids. Abrupt halt, rein-back not very supple. Passage improves on the two circles, but the horse constantly swishes his tail and the rider tugs at the reins. The first steps of the third piaffe are quite brilliant but immediately the impulsion is lost again.

Judge C: 274 (23), H: 289 (16), M: 322 (11), E: 292 (21), B: 303 (20), Total: 1480 (91).

John Winnett on Reinald. Good halt and move-off. Extended trot very hasty. Medium canter lacking impulsion. Flying change is well forward. Hesitant transition into the collected trot. Extended trot again hasty; good medium trot. Alternating rein-back and forward is not very supple. Good medium trot and transition into the collected trot. In the half pass to the left the horse comes behind the bit; the same in the half pass to the right. Insufficient lateral flexion. Extended walk is hasty and does not cover ground to the front. Good transitions into the medium and collected walk. Half pirouette to the right is good. Insufficient activity of the hind quarters in the pirouette to the left. First passage flat; faltering transition into the piaffe, which is merely outlined. Second transition into the piaffe fails again. The extended canter is well begun, but after a few bounds the tempo is decreased to the collected canter. In the half pass zigzags the horse is behind the bit and the bounds of canter lack forward urge. Extended canter consists of a few bounds only and is too soon reduced to the collected canter. The rhythm of the canter is lost in the pirouette to the left; the pirouette to the right is somewhat better. Flying changes at two strides are good; faults in the flying changes at every stride. The collected canter before the halt is a four-beat pace. Good halt. Strike-off into the canter instead of moving off into the passage. Irregular passage on the circles; transition into the piaffe fails.

Judge C: 279 (21), H: 283 (22), M: 308 (19), E: 283 (24), B: 305 (17), Total: 1458 (103).

Lois Stephens on Fasching. Halt with the hind legs not engaged. Horse does not move on immediately into the collected trot. Strike-off into the canter during the extended trot. The horse comes behind the bit, which fault is remedied after X only. At the medium canter the horse is behind the bit and swaying. No gain of ground in the extended trot. The rider leans her upper part back. Medium trot is presented exactly like the extended trot. The horse is very much behind the bit. He violently agitates his tail in the exercise of alternating rein-back and going forward. Some hovering steps at the collected trot before the half pass. The half pass is imprecisely laid out and, to the left, with insufficient lateral position. Collected walk with inadequate collection. The extended walk is hasty and does not gain ground to the front. Half pirouette to the right with inactive hind quarters. The same in the pirouette to the left, which is too large. Irregular steps in the first passage, the hind quarters are not active. The horse becomes resistant and bucks. After this incident the piaffe

is surprisingly good. Extended canter without gain of
ground. The horse comes behind the bit in the half pass
zigzags, which are very imprecisely designed. Pirouette to
the right with irregular bounds of canter. Faults in the
flying changes at two strides which come completely off
the track. The horse arrives at the long side of the arena
twelve meters before the prescribed mark. Flying changes
at every stride are good at the beginning but then become increasingly shorter. The horse sticks his tongue
out. He shies in the middle of the short side and the rider
is unable to perform the required medium canter. Good
halt on the center line but not on the prescribed spot.
Good transition into the passage from the rein-back; however, several irregular steps in the passage.
Judge C: 274 (23), H: 278 (25), M: 277 (30), E: 254
(31), B: 262 (32), Total: 1345 (141).

*Canada*
Christilot Hansen on Armagnac. Good entry and halt.
Regular extended trot which gains ground to the front. At
the flying changes at the medium canter the horse throws
his hind quarters slightly to the side. Good transition into
the collected trot. Extended trot very good. Very impulsive medium trot. The rein-back not very supple in the
exercise of alternating rein-back and forward. The prescribed number of steps is not observed. Distinct difference between the medium and collected trot. Half
pass to the left not very supple, the rider leans her upper
part back. The same in the half pass to the right. Collected walk is not sufficiently collected; extended walk is
regular. The horse whinnies twice. Half pirouette to the
right with little activity of the hind quarters. In the half

pirouette to the left the hind legs move even less. Slight hesitation before the first passage but then the movement is improving. Piaffe with little brilliance. Slight disorder in the transition into the second piaffe. Clear difference of speed between the extended and the collected canter. Half pass zigzags are irregular. The extended canter does not cover ground to the front. In the pirouette to the left the rhythm of the canter is lost; the pirouette to the right is not good either. In the flying changes at the canter at two strides the horse's hind legs do not always make a full stride. Faults in the flying changes at every stride. Good transition from the medium to the collected canter. At the halt the hind quarters do not step under the body of the horse. Hasty rein-back. In the passage the horse should lift his legs higher. The transition into the piaffe fails and so does the last piaffe.

Judge C: 303 (15), H: 300 (14), M: 344 (6), E: 326 (4), B: 342 (3), Total: 1615 (42).

Lorraine Stubbs on Venezuela. Abrupt halt, the rider's upper part leans back. The horse does not move off directly from the halt. Irregular steps at the extended trot. Crooked strike-off into the canter. Good medium canter and flying change. Good extended trot; however, the rider leans back very much. No difference at the transition into the medium trot. In the exercise of alternating rein-back and forward the horse comes very much behind the bit in the rein-back. The prescribed number of steps is not observed. The collected trot is insufficiently collected. Half pass to the left is insufficient; the rider leans her upper part back and wags her head. Collected walk is insufficiently collected. The extended walk does not gain ground but becomes hasty. The rider not only leans her upper part back but also grips the horse's body with her calves. Differences of tempo at the walk are not noticeable. The half pirouette to the right without any activity of the hind quarters. The walk becomes a pure amble. In the half pirouette to the left the hind quarters are not very active either. In the turn at the passage the hind quarters swing to the outside of the arena. Both the transitions into the piaffe and the piaffe itself fail. The same at the second piaffe. In the extended and collected canters the horse becomes crooked. Half pass zigzags and extended canter are sufficient. In the pirouette to the left the rhythm of the canter is lost completely. The horse is spun around for the pirouette to the right. The flying changes at two strides are executed well forward but with the hind quarters slightly thrown to the side. Good flying changes at every stride. Good halt and rein-back, but the passage is not begun from the rein-back. The passage is without brilliance. What strikes most is the balancing action of the rider's upper part. The transition into the piaffe fails and this movement is just outlined. Final halt with the hind legs not under the horse.

Judge C: 263 (28), H: 270 (30), M: 296 (27), E: 273 (28), B: 277 (30), Total: 1379 (143).

Cynthia Neal on Bonne Année. Good entry and supple halt, but the hind legs are not sufficiently engaged. Regular extended trot. Good strike-off into the canter. At the flying change the horse does not take a full stride with the hind leg. Extended trot sufficient. No difference to the medium trot. The rider leans her upper part back. Alternate rein-back and forward with fluent sequence of steps. Transition into the trot not very supple. The half pass lacks impulsion. Collected walk is inadequately collected.

21. G. Fischer on Wald—Silver medal 1960

22. Mr. Boldt on Remus—Silver medal 1964

23. H. Chammartin on Woermann—Gold medal 1964

24. Mr. Kisimow on Ikhor—Gold medal 1968

25. Mr. Klimke on Dux—Bronze medal 1968

26. Mrs. Linsenhoff on Piaff—Gold medal 1972 (Bronze medal 1956 on Adular)

27. Mrs. Petuschkowa on Pepel—Silver medal 1972

28. Mr. Neckermann on Venetia—Bronze medal 1972 (Bronze medal 1960 on Asbach and Silver medal 1968 on Mariano)

The extended walk is hasty and does not gain ground to the front. It is impossible to see any difference of tempo at the walk. Both half pirouettes with little activity of the hind legs. The horse hangs his tongue out. Passage is cadenced but hasty. The transition into the piaffe fails; the piaffe is very weak. In the collected canter and the exercises in that pace which follow the horse comes behind the bit. In both pirouettes the rhythm of the canter is lost. In the flying changes at two strides the horse throws his hind quarters to the side. Faults in the changes at every stride. The horse is very much behind the bit and hangs his tongue out. Halt with the hind legs not engaged, nevertheless a good rein-back. Good move-off into the passage. The passage on the circles is very irregular. The rider pulls her heels up and constantly kicks the horse's sides with her legs. She leans her upper part back and tugs at the reins. In spite of all her efforts the horse's hind legs do not step under his body.

Judge C: 267 (27), H: 274 (27), M: 283 (29), E: 293 (20), B: 307 (16), Total: 1424 (119).

### Denmark

Aksel Mikkelsen on Talisman. Halt with the hind legs not under the horse. The horse does not remain immobile and anticipates the move-off into the trot. Extended trot impulsive, good transition into the canter; regular medium canter with distinct change of tempo into the collected canter. Somewhat hesitant transition into the collected trot. Extended trot covers much ground to the front. In the rein-back-forward-rein-back the prescribed number of steps is not observed. Slight disturbance in the transition from the medium to the collected trot. Half pass to the left is not very supple, somewhat better to the right. The extended walk does not gain ground; the horse constantly swishes his tail. At the walk some pace-like steps. Impulsive extended canter and distinct transition into the collected canter. Good half pass zigzags. Extended canter does not cover sufficient ground. Good pirouette to the left; pirouette to the right is very good. Very good flying changes at two strides; the flying changes at every stride are without a fault but do not cover sufficient ground to the front. Consequently, this exercise comes to an end at X. The rider's seat is correct and his use of the aids discreet. Good halt. One step is missing in the rein-back. Good move-off into the passage, which, however, is somewhat hasty. Very good transition into the piaffe and the piaffe itself is excellent in rhythm and suppleness. One of the best piaffes that we have seen so far. (That is, the first riders of each national team as observed and discussed up to this point.)

Judge C: 313 (9), H: 319 (8), M: 313 (14), E: 324 (6), B: 328 (10), Total: 1597 (47).

Charlotte Ingemann on Souliman. The horse comes to a halt after several intermediate steps at the walk. His hind legs do not step under his body. He does not move off into the trot from the halt. Impulsive extended trot well gaining ground to the front. Crooked strike-off into the canter. Medium canter without forward urge. No difference to the collected canter. Extended trot again very good; however, practically no difference to the medium trot. At the halt the horse's left hind leg does not step under his body. Resistance at the rein-back; the exercise of alternating rein-back and forward is not supple. Distinct difference of tempo between medium and collected trot. In both half passes the horse does not adopt sufficient lateral position. Collected walk is inadequately collected. The extended walk does gain ground to the front but is too hasty in rhythm. The other changes of tempo at the walk are distinctly noticeable. Both half pirouettes are good. Good transition into the passage, which, however, is too hasty in rhythm. The transition into the piaffe and the piaffe itself are flat. Insufficient transition into the second piaffe; the horse swishes his tail and steps backwards. Good changes of tempo at the canter. In the half pass zigzags the impulsion is lost and the exercise is performed at a four-beat canter. Distinct extended canter; again four beats in the collected canter. The pirouette to the left is sufficient, the horse throws himself into the pirouette to the right and is spun around. Flying changes at two strides and at every stride executed without fault but not sufficiently forward. Towards the end of the exercise there is again a four-beat canter, which continues until the halt. At the halt the horse's hind quarters are not engaged. Irregular steps at the passage. The transition into the piaffe fails and the piaffe is not more than a bad balancé. At the final halt the horse does not engage his hind legs.

Judge C: 291 (19), H: 288 (19), M: 314 (13), E: 278 (27), B: 304 (19), Total: 1475 (97).

Ulla Petersen on Chigwell. Impulsive extended trot. At the flying changes at the medium canter the horse does not take a full stride with the hind legs. Irregular tempo in both half passes. Extended walk does not gain ground and is hasty. Collected walk somewhat irregular in the sequence of steps. Both half pirouettes are good. Passage and piaffe as well as the transitions are quite good. Extended canter does not cover sufficient ground to the front. Pirouette to the left is good; that to the right is too large. Faults in the flying changes at the canter at two strides; the flying changes at every stride are not performed with sufficient forward movement. In the final piaffe irregular steps.

Judge C: 307 (13), H: 301 (13), M: 306 (20), E: 319 (9), B: 301 (21), Total: 1534 (76).

*Individual riders*

Patrick Le Rolland (France) on Cramique. Good entry and halt. Move-off into the trot is not executed from the halt. There are uneven steps at the collected trot. At the extended trot there is an obvious lameness of one hind leg which is also noticeable at the medium trot and probably the reason for the jolting bounds of canter. The exercise of the alternating rein-back and forward is very irregular and with hasty steps at times. The lameness persists. It is even noticeable to the non-initiated observer, especially on straight lines. The expert wonders why the rider does not give up, bringing his performance prematurely to an end. It is even more incomprehensible that there is no reaction whatsoever from the jury that continues to score the rider's performance. The exercises at the walk are very irregular; the extended walk distinctly reveals the difference in the length of the steps. The lameness that was obvious at the trot becomes even more visible at the passage. A presentation which causes much uneasiness and disapproval in all grandstands.

Judge C: 262 (29), H: 332 (7), M: 306 (20), E: 270 (29), B: 281 (28), Total: 1451 (113).

Silvio M. de Rezende (Brazil) on Othelo. The horse's hind legs are not engaged at the halt. Extended trot does not cover ground to the front. Crooked strike-off into the canter. Flat medium canter; no difference to the collected canter. Extended trot again without much gain of ground, not very supple, and there is no difference to the medium trot. The number of steps is not observed in the exercise of rein-back and forward. In the half pass to the left irregular lateral position. To the right the horse takes insufficient lateral position (not parallel to the long side of the arena). Good extended walk and distinct changes of tempo. In both half pirouettes the hind quarters remain inactive, the horse's feet literally stick to the ground. Flat passage; irregular piaffe. The extended canter does not gain ground to the front and there is no forward drive. Half pass zigzags are not very supple. Extended canter again insufficient. Both pirouettes are sufficient. Flying changes at the canter at two strides do not gain ground to the front; the same at the flying changes at every stride in which there are several faults. At the halt the horse does not step under his body with his left hind leg. Irregular steps at the passage. In the final piaffe the horse swishes his tail.

Judge C: 262 (29), H: 279 (24), M: 304 (22), E: 289 (23), B: 297 (25), Total: 1431 (123).

Kikuko Inoue (Japan) on Don Carlos. The horse does not remain immobile at the halt. The extended trot is without forward drive and with irregular steps. The horse is crooked at the canter on the left lead. Again uneven steps at the extended trot and no difference to the medium trot. Crooked at the halt. Resistance at the rein-back. Uneven steps at the collected trot. In the half pass to the left inadequate lateral position and irregular steps. The same in the half pass to the right. Extended walk is hasty and with irregular steps, it does not cover ground to the front. Uneven steps at the collected walk. In the half pirouette to the right the hind quarters remain inactive. The half pirouette to the left is somewhat better. Piaffe very irregular in rhythm; in the passage the horse's hind quarters begin to sway. Half pass zigzags are not very supple; the rhythm of the canter is lost. In the pirouette to the right the horse is spun around. The impulsion is lost in the flying changes at two strides and at every stride. There are several faults. Disturbance at the halt and rein-back. Irregular passage, the circles are not round.

Judge C: 258 (32), H: 252 (33), M: 270 (32), E: 264 (30), B: 269 (31), Total: 1313 (158).

## RIDE-OFF FOR THE INDIVIDUAL MEDALISTS

*Ivan Kisimov on Ikhor* (U.S.S.R.)

Entry at a four-beat canter. Hind legs of the horse not engaged at the halt. Departure into the trot does not come from the halt. The extended trot gains ground well, but the horse is behind the bit. The rider has the tread of his left stirrup up against his heel. Fluent half pass to the right. At C strike-off into canter instead of extended trot. Insufficient extended trot. Distinct collected trot. Second extended trot does not gain ground to the front, the horse is behind the bit, his mouth is open. Half pass to the left is fluent. Collected walk with lively active steps. In the first piaffe the horse moves backwards for a few steps, but then the piaffe is very active and rhythmic. First passage very brilliant and regular. The rhythm is lost in the transi-

tion into the piaffe. Second passage again very brilliant
and regular. Extended trot with some uneven steps. The
action of the horse's front legs indicates greater extension
than can be produced by the hind legs. The extended
walk does not gain sufficient ground to the front. The
rider deviates from the diagonal and does not ride with
precision through the corners of the arena. Flying
changes at the canter at two strides are good. In the
flying changes at every stride the horse comes behind the
bit and swishes his tail. There is one fault. The rhythm of
the canter is lost in the pirouette to the right. The number
of flying changes at every stride is inferior to that prescribed in the test. The rhythm of the canter is lost again
in the pirouette to the left. Very impulsive extended
canter. The horse comes very much behind the bit in the
transition from the collected canter into the collected
trot. In the last passage the horse does not lift his legs
high enough; he becomes hasty. Very good final piaffe
and halt.
Judge C: 224 (3), H: 243 (2), M: 244 (4), E: 223 (6),
B: 225 (5), Total: 1159 (20).

*Liselott Linsenhoff on Piaff* (F.R.G.)
Hind legs not engaged at the halt. Several irregular steps
at the collected trot, which is insufficiently collected. Extended trot is impulsive and covers ground to the front.
In the transition into the collected trot the strides become
slower instead of shorter. The changes of tempo at the
trot are not very clear, hardly to be distinguished. First
piaffe and passage are good. The transition into the second piaffe, however, is not good and the piaffe itself

rather irregular. Good second passage. Extended trot is rather hasty and irregular in tempo. Extended walk gains sufficient ground to the front. Good flying changes at two strides; one fault in the flying changes at every stride. The rhythm of the canter is lost in the pirouette to the right; the rider spins the horse around. One fault in the flying changes at every stride on the center line. The pirouette to the left fails completely. The extended canter gains sufficient ground to the front. Very hesitant transition into the collected canter. In the passage the hind legs do not step sufficiently under the body of the horse.

Judge C: 232 (1), H: 257 (1), M: 245 (2), E: 254 (1), B: 241 (1), Total: 1229 (6).

*Ulla Hakansson on Ajax* (Sweden)

Good entry and halt. Extended trot very regular and covering ground to the front. Distinct transition into the collected trot. Half pass to the right very fluent. Distinct changes of tempo and very fluent transitions in the alternating extended and collected trot on short lines. Half pass to the left not very supple. The first piaffe is very regular in rhythm. Good transition into the passage. In the passage, however, the horse takes some shorter strides with one hind leg. Supple transitions into the second piaffe and second passage. In the passage again some shorter strides with one hind leg. Very good transition into the extended trot, which gains good ground to the front. Hasty extended walk which does not cover ground. Distinct transition into the collected walk. Very good strike-off into the canter. Flying changes at two strides impulsive and well forward. The same in the flying changes at every stride. Very good pirouette to the right. Flying changes on the center line well forward but with one fault. The rhythm of the canter is lost in the pirouette to the left. Extended canter might be more brilliant and gain more ground to the front. Supple transition into the collected trot. Very brilliant passage. After the transition into the final piaffe the activity of the hind quarters declines. Improves again towards the final halt.

Judge C: 226 (2), H: 233 (5), M: 215 (11), E: 227 (5), B: 225 (5), Total: 1126 (28).

*Christilot Hansen on Armagnac* (Canada)

Left hind leg not engaged at the halt. Very brilliant extended trot. The rider's upper part leans back. Good half pass to the right and distinct difference between extended and collected trot on very short lines. Supple half pass to the left. The transition into the walk is not executed at the prescribed mark (at S instead of at H). First piaffe with irregular steps. Hesitant transition into the passage. The passage becomes too superficial towards the end. Very impulsive extended trot which covers good ground to the front. Extended walk too hasty; it does not gain ground. Irregular steps towards the end of this exercise. Good strike-off into the canter. The horse throws his hind quarters to the side in the flying changes at two strides. One fault. The flying changes at every stride do not gain ground towards the end of the diagonal. The rider pulls her heels up. The rhythm of the canter is lost in the pirouette to the right. Flying changes on the center line are not supple. The pirouette to the left is better. Last passage begins well but towards the end becomes too superficial.

Transition into the piaffe is not very supple. Uneven steps in the piaffe.

Judge C: 204 (10), H: 229 (6), M: 211 (12), E: 219 (8), B: 218 (10), Total: 1081 (46).

*Aksel Mikkelsen on Talisman* (Denmark)
Entry at a four-beat canter. The horse's hind legs do not step under his body at the halt. Departure into the trot does not come from the halt. In the extended trot the horse does not lengthen his frame, his steps do not cover ground. Fluent half pass to the right. The extended trot is begun too soon, the horse strikes off into the canter and the transition into the collected trot fails. The following transition into the extended trot is again disturbed by a strike-off into the canter. In the half pass to the left the horse is behind the bit. The departure into the first piaffe fails, the horse becomes crooked and swishes his tail. The passage is rather flat but sufficient. In the transition into the second piaffe the horse comes behind the bit and cannot adapt to the rhythm. In the second passage the horse takes several shorter strides with one hind leg. Extended walk is regular and covers ground to the front. Good flying changes at the canter. Flying changes at every stride on the diagonal are not sufficiently forward. Sufficient pirouette to the right. Good flying changes on the center line and following pirouette to the left. Extended canter does not gain ground. Difficulties during the transition into the collected trot. Last passage somewhat hasty and not very brilliant. Uneven steps in the final piaffe, the horse sometimes steps backwards.

Judge C: 200 (11), H: 210 (10), M: 222 (9), E: 208 (11), B: 220 (9), Total: 1060 (50).

*Iwan Kalita on Tarif* (U.S.S.R.)

Good entry and halt; however, the horse does not remain immobile. Regular extended trot which gains ground well to the front. Very fluent half pass to the right. Distinct changes of tempo at the trot. Half pass to the left is also good. Piaffe is executed on the spot, but the horse sometimes steps backwards. Passage with very active hind quarters, supple transition into the piaffe, which is flat. The prescribed lines are very imprecisely followed. Extended trot is regular and covers ground. The extended walk does not gain ground. There are hasty steps before the strike-off into the canter. The flying changes at two strides and at every stride are regular in rhythm and well forward. Very good pirouette to the right and very good flying changes on the center line. The rhythm of the canter is lost in the pirouette to the left. Impulsive extended canter which covers ground to the front. Distinct transition into the collected canter. Last passage is very brilliant and regular with supple transition into the piaffe, which, however, loses the rhythm.

Judge C: 219 (5), H: 226 (7), M: 238 (5), E: 223 (6), B: 224 (7), Total: 1130 (30).

*Karin Schlüter on Liostro* (F.R.G.)

Very good entry and halt. Extended trot is regular and covers ground to the front. The horse swishes his tail in the half pass to the right. Distinct changes of tempo at the trot. In the half pass to the left the horse does not maintain a regular tempo. Before the first piaffe the horse launches himself into a half pirouette and the piaffe fails. First passage is impulsive and regular. Transition into the piaffe and the piaffe itself is very weak. Second passage again brilliant. Extended trot is impulsive and covers ground. Extended walk is sufficient but hasty at times. Supple transition into the canter. One fault in each of the flying changes at two strides and at every stride. The horse does not take a full stride with the hind leg. The rhythm of the canter is lost in the pirouette to the right. Following flying changes at every stride are without fault. The rhythm of the canter is again lost in the pirouette to the left. Extended canter gains ground to the front; distinct transition into the collected canter. Passage on the center line very expressive, especially at the beginning of the exercise.

Judge C: 205 (9), H: 217 (8), M: 230 (8), E: 233 (3), B: 228 (4), Total: 1113 (32).

*Ninna Swaab on Casanova* (Sweden)

Good entry and halt. Departure into the trot directly from the halt. Extended trot somewhat flat. Hesitant movement in the half pass to the right; the horse comes behind the bit. Distinct differences of tempo between the extended and collected trot and vice versa. Half pass to the left not very supple. First piaffe with very regular steps and expressive first passage. In the second piaffe insufficient activity of the hind quarters; it is some sort of balancé. In the following passage the rider upsets the horse, which becomes crooked. Uneven steps in the extended trot. The extended walk does not cover ground to the front. Two faults in the flying changes at two strides; there is no fault in the flying changes at every stride, but the horse violently swishes his tail. The rhythm of the canter is lost in the pirouette to the right. The flying changes on the center line are without forward drive. In the pirouette to the left the rhythm of the canter is again lost. Extended canter covers ground to the front. Supple transition into the collected canter and collected trot. Last passage is flat and there is no regular rhythm in the final piaffe.

Judge C: 210 (8), H: 201 (12), M: 234 (6), E: 210 (10), B: 212 (11), Total: 1067 (47).

*Elena Petuschkowa on Pepel* (U.S.S.R.)

Good entry; hind legs of the horse not engaged at the halt. The horse does not remain immobile. Extended trot does not gain ground to the front. Half pass to the right without forward urge. Distinct differences of tempo at the trot. Half pass to the left is hesitant. The rider constantly has the tread of her stirrup up against her heel. Collected walk is hasty. In the first piaffe the horse violently swishes his tail. The following passage is very expressive; the second piaffe is regular. The rider performs the exercises very imprecisely. For instance, in order to arrive at L she turns long before reaching V. Extended trot is hasty and does not gain ground to the front. The strides at the extended walk are hasty and not long enough. Flying changes at two strides well forward but with one fault. Very good flying changes at every stride. The rhythm is lost in the pirouette to the right. In the following flying changes at every stride the horse does not take a full stride with the hind leg at one change. Pirouette to the left is good. There is a distinct difference between extended and collected canter. In the last passage the horse takes a shorter stride with one hind leg. Final piaffe begins well but then the horse steps backwards.

Judge C: 220 (4), H: 243 (2), M: 257 (1), E: 230 (4), B: 235 (2), Total: 1185 (13).

*Josef Neckermann on Venetia* (F.R.G.)
Halt after intermediate steps at the walk. The hind quarters are not engaged. Extended trot regular and with gain of ground to the front. Half pass to the right is not very supple. Extended trot is executed with hasty steps that do not cover ground. The rider's upper part leans back. Half pass to the left is better. At the collected walk the horse paces. In the first piaffe the horse steps backwards with the left hind leg. First passage is flat. Transition into the piaffe is not very supple. The horse does not remain straight. The exercises are very imprecisely ridden. Second passage is better. Extended trot is hasty and does not gain ground. The first strides at the collected walk are again a pure amble, then the movement improves. Extended walk is hasty and does not cover ground to the front. Good flying changes at two strides which, however, deviate badly from the diagonal. Very short bounds of canter in the flying changes at every stride; that is, they are not enough forward. The pirouette to the right is small but with loss of rhythm of the canter. Flying changes on the center line are good. Good pirouette to the left. Very impulsive extended canter. In the last passage uneven steps. Good final piaffe.
Judge C: 211 (7), H: 240 (4), M: 245 (2), E: 247 (2), B: 234 (3), Total: 1177 (18).

*Maud von Rosen on Lucky Boy* (Sweden)
Hind legs of the horse are not engaged at the halt. Extended trot is very impulsive and gaining ground to the

front. In the transition into the collected trot the rhythm is lost. Very fluent half pass to the right. Distinct changes of tempo at the trot. Hesitant half pass to the left. First piaffe is weak. First passage with little impulsion. The transition into the second piaffe fails and the piaffe itself is not performed. Prescribed turns at the second passage are imprecisely ridden. Second passage is very flat. Distinct transition into the extended trot; however, some uneven steps in the center of the diagonal. Extended walk is good but the rider moves her upper part forwards and back, spoiling the good impression. Flying changes at two strides are well forward; the same with the flying changes at every stride, but the rider deviates from the diagonal. She is sliding about in the saddle. The rhythm of the canter is lost in the pirouette to the right on the center line. Good flying changes at every stride. The rhythm is again lost in the pirouette to the left. Extended canter is impulsive and covers ground to the front. Distinct transition into the collected canter. The first steps at the following passage are very brilliant, but soon the impulsion dies down. No regular rhythm in the final piaffe.

Judge C: 215 (6), H: 215 (9), M: 219 (10), E: 218 (9), B: 221 (8), Total: 1088 (42).

*Hilda Lorna Johnstone on El Farruco* (Great Britain)
Halt after intermediate steps of walk; the horse comes above the bit. Collected trot too hasty. Hasty extended trot which does not gain ground to the front. Some hovering steps at the collected trot. Hesitant half pass to the right. Hovering steps at the moment of change of tempo at the trot. Rider constantly has the tread of the stirrup up against her heel. Irregular steps at the half pass to the

left. Imprecise riding of figures and lines at the walk. In
the first piaffe the horse steps backwards. First passage
brilliant. The transition into the piaffe fails and this exercise is merely outlined. Second passage full of impulsion.
Hasty steps at the following extended trot, which does
not cover ground. The horse merely extends his front legs
without adequate action of the hind legs. Flying changes
at two strides and at every stride are well forward and
straight. Pirouette to the right is small but with loss of
rhythm of the canter. Flying changes at every stride on
the center line are straight and well forward. In the pirouette to the left the rhythm of the canter dies down. Extended trot gains ground to the front; good transition into
the collected trot. Passage is very hasty and without brilliance. Last piaffe is merely indicated by a restless stepping about on the spot.
Judge C: 190 (12), H: 205 (11), M: 232 (7), E: 203
(12), B: 206 (12), Total: 1036 (54).

So much about the performances of the riders and their
evaluation by the judges. This summary also gives the
order in which the contestants were classified by the various judges in the scores awarded. The order of the competitors, namely the place mark, is even more interesting
for the observer, as it provides a better and quicker over-
all estimation than the total of scores awarded for the
different groups of exercises in the test. It is far less important how many marks the judge awards to a rider, for
the total of marks does not reveal anything at all about
the rider's abilities, as may be seen from the summary of
the Grand Prix above. Two judges with the same total of
scores may put one and the same rider in two different
places.

Munich, with thirty-three riders competing, had the second largest number of Olympic participants in the Grand Prix de Dressage (thirty-six competed in the dressage test of the 1956 Olympic Games). This positive development is balanced, however, by a number of negative facts briefly enumerated here. Improvements in performances did not become obvious to the degree that might be expected considering the increasing interest in the sport of riding in the past twenty-seven years, which should have provided a larger basis from which top riders might have developed. The standard of dressage in the thirties was far from being reached. This may be said not only about piaffe and passage and the other airs of Haute Ecole but also and above all about the fundamentals of training which should be expected from any good riding horse. This deficiency in the foundation of schooling was quite obviously the cause of most faults which struck the observer throughout the test.

At the Olympic Games we expect that the best riders will present to the enthusiasts of horsemanship, who are so numerous today, and to youth, especially, the goal that even the average rider should strive for, namely—and it bears repeating once more—the well-trained horse, which conveys to the rider on his back the proverbial greatest happiness on earth. This would make the Olympic rider an ideal fixed in the minds of the people. He would thus be awarded a prize certainly more precious than many a controversial Olympic medal. He would set an example and a goal for equitation. Furthermore, by demonstratively mastering the fundamentals of riding he would return to the right path many a fledgling rider who, as soon as mounted, dreams about piaffe and Haute Ecole.

As an impartial observer, I regret to state, however, that there was not much of an Olympic spark in the Grand Prix de Dressage in Munich. For the presentations were not much different from those to be seen at any great international horse show in which, among others, there are riders who want to try out their horses for the first time in the more difficult classes.

Passing before the mind's eye the performances seen in the Nymphenburger Park, it strikes the observer how often, above all, the riders failed to present their horses in pure paces, beginning with the walk and on up to the airs of Haute Ecole. How rare were freedom and regularity in the different tempi of the walk, especially in the extended walk, in which the horse should take long, far-reaching strides covering ground to the front. How often a horse was near pacing and ended up by presenting a pure amble because the natural movement was lost through all sorts of artificial devices. Frequently the extended trot degenerated into some sort of running gait with hasty steps instead of appearing as a movement full of impulsion and gaining ground to the front. And where was the exciting extended canter that for thousands of years had been the culmination of riding? Hardly one of the riders performed the half pirouettes at the walk and the full pirouettes at the canter without difficulty. The open mouth of the horse with the tongue pulled up, the swishing tail, and other bad habits were as commonly seen as the too noticeable use of the rider's seat and rein aids.

The cause of all the divergencies in the evaluations is not to be sought in the judges alone. Certainly "the best riders of the world" deserve to be judged by the best judges of the world. On the other hand, the judges are entitled to see an honest if not perfect presentation. It is asking too much of a judge in an Olympic dressage test to have to evaluate horses and riders whose standard of riding is in no way equal to the demands of the test. In a test of that standard it is the result of completed training that should be presented. Instead, many riders—and the federations delegating them—quite obviously adopted the "somehow it will work" attitude. This, however, does not serve a good turn either to the individual rider or to his country and least of all to the sport of riding.

Maybe some readers will think this report about the various rides in Munich rather relentless and uncompromising. Yet it was not dictated by the mere joy of criticising. Giving praise would not only be easier but also far more gratifying. This report is meant to give advice, to point to the cause of the problems, and to show the way to be taken in order to bring dressage riding again nearer perfection.

There is an interesting observation with which to conclude the review of the riders at the dressage tests of the Olympic Games. It is to remind us that in the sport of riding as in so many other spheres there is a constant up and down. The 1952 riders of the Soviet Union participated in the Olympic Grand Prix de Dressage in Helsinki for the first time. They placed in the second half of the field of riders. In 1960 in Rome, however, they won the gold medal; in 1964 in Tokyo, they won the bronze medal in both the team and the individual tests. In 1968 in Mexico the Soviet riders were awarded the silver medal for the team and the gold medal for the individual rider. Munich in 1972 brought them the gold medal for the team and the silver medal for the individual rider. In other words, they moved up to take a place among the top nations in dressage, ranking with the Federal Republic of Germany and Sweden—a place that once belonged to France, Denmark, U.S.A., Netherlands, and Switzerland. Even though the last-mentioned countries, France excepted, delegated teams to Munich, they were by no means among the better half of the field of riders. There was a total absence of riders from those nations that of old were the strongholds of dressage, such as Norway or Hungary, Czechoslovakia and Austria, though this time the Games were held in the center of Europe, right at their front door, so to speak. Nor did the only representative of France bring to Munich the slightest trace of the bygone splendour of dressage riding in his country.

And now a few comments about the method of judging and the judges themselves, whose performance was criticised by the press of practically all competing nations. We have already discussed the development of and the attempts to improve the system of judging during the sixty years since the inclusion of this branch of the sport in the Olympic Games. In Munich, at last, the long-time demand made by equestrian circles was granted. The judges were no longer to compare and to correct the results of their marks before the publication of the scores, dragging out the time of the dressage competition by long-winded discussions. They were to announce their evaluations immediately after the scores had been added. Thus each judge was openly taking the responsibility for his judging. However, the term "system of open judging" is pertinent to a limited degree only. For at best it was possible for a rider to consult his own score sheets but none of the others, which would reveal how the individual marks produced the final result. The "comparison of the results of the principal test" on the following pages will provide a clear picture of the differentiations in the evaluations of the judges.

For six riders the difference between the highest and the lowest place marks given by the different judges is from two to four places. Such differences might be tolerated considering the numerous groups of exercises to be judged. This tolerance, however, is no longer admissible for those cases in which the difference amounts to six and seven places, as occurred with three riders, and to eight places as with four riders. Moreover, two riders were respectively scored with differences of nine and eleven places, and for one rider differences amounted to fourteen, sixteen, twenty, twenty-one, and twenty-two places.

In the face of such facts it is difficult to speak about a uniform concept of dressage riding among the judges in Munich. When comparing the sum of the marks, the contrasts do not become so obvious at first sight. They leap to the eye, however, when ranging the riders according to their place marks. Of course, the individual judge's score sheet for one rider may very well differ from the same rider's score sheets from the other judges. After all, there is a choice of scores. Good performances may be rewarded by ten to eight marks, sufficient ones by seven to five, and insufficient ones by four to one. As a result, a severe evaluation is never of disadvantage when determining the winner according to place marks, provided, of course, that all riders are judged in the same manner and in just relation to each other.

No allowance should be made for riders of one's own country or for friends, nor should opponents of one's countrymen or riders who do not appeal to the judge be judged differently. It is a vital part of the judge's charac-

## COMPARISON OF THE RESULTS OF THE PRINCIPAL TEST

| Rider | Horse | Nation | The total of the scores of all judges lies between the bonus points: | C: Nyblaeus Sweden | H: Herrera Mexico | M: de Breuil France | E: Pollay F.R.G. | B: Pot Netherlands | Difference between highest and lowest place marks | Placing according to the total of scores | Placing according to place marks |
|---|---|---|---|---|---|---|---|---|---|---|---|
| Liselott Linsenhoff | Piaff | F.R.G. | 368-326 | 4 | 1 | 7 | 1 | 1 | 6 | 1 | 2 |
| Elena Petuschkowa | Pepel | U.S.S.R. | 365-323 | 1 | 2 | 1 | 7 | 2 | 6 | 2 | 1 |
| Josef Neckermann | Venetia | F.R.G. | 355-314 | 8 | 4 | 4 | 2 | 5 | 6 | 3 | 4 |
| Ivan Kisimov | Ikhor | U.S.S.R. | 357-322 | 6 | 5 | 2 | 3 | 5 | 4 | 4 | 3 |
| Ulla Hakansson | Ajax | Sweden | 357-311 | 2 | 3 | 15 | 8 | 9 | 13 | 5 | 6 |
| Iwan Kalita | Tarif | U.S.S.R. | 338-322 | 4 | 6 | 8 | 5 | 12 | 8 | 6 | 5 |
| Ninna Swaab | Casanova | Sweden | 341-313 | 7 | 9 | 9 | 9 | 4 | 5 | 7 | 7 |
| Christilot Hansen | Armagnac | Canada | 344-300 | 15 | 14 | 6 | 4 | 3 | 12 | 8 | 9 |
| Karin Schlüter | Liostro | F.R.G. | 347-289 | 3 | 16 | 4 | 9 | 8 | 13 | 9 | 8 |
| Aksel Mikkelsen | Talisman | Denmark | 328-313 | 9 | 8 | 14 | 6 | 10 | 8 | 10 | 10 |
| Maud von Rosen | Lucky Boy | Sweden | 332-304 | 9 | 12 | 10 | 13 | 13 | 4 | 11 | 11 |
| Hilda Lorna Johnstone | El Farruco | Great Britain | 349-300 | 13 | 11 | 3 | 12 | 23 | 20 | 12 | 12 |

| Gerhard Brockmüller | Marios | D.R.G. | 335-281 | 9 | 23 | 18 | 14 | 7 | 16 | 13 | 13 |
|---|---|---|---|---|---|---|---|---|---|---|---|
| Ulla Petersen | Chigwell | Denmark | 319-301 | 13 | 13 | 20 | 9 | 21 | 12 | 14 | 16 |
| Christine Stuckelberger | Granat | Switzerland | 311-296 | 18 | 10 | 15 | 16 | 14 | 8 | 15 | 14 |
| Wolfgang Müller | Semafor | D.R.G. | 315-284 | 12 | 21 | 12 | 14 | 15 | 9 | 16 | 15 |
| Horst Köhler | Imanuel | D.R.G. | 328-273 | 17 | 20 | 31 | 17 | 10 | 21 | 17 | 19 |
| Edith Master | Dahlwitz | U.S.A. | 322-274 | 23 | 16 | 11 | 21 | 20 | 12 | 18 | 18 |
| Annie van Doorne | Pericles | Netherlands | 311-274 | 23 | 16 | 15 | 17 | 17 | 8 | 18 | 17 |
| Charlotte Ingemann | Souliman | Denmark | 314-278 | 19 | 19 | 13 | 27 | 19 | 14 | 20 | 20 |
| Hermann Dur | Sod | Switzerland | 301-271 | 16 | 29 | 25 | 19 | 25 | 13 | 21 | 24 |
| John Winnett, Jr. | Reinald | U.S.A. | 308-279 | 21 | 22 | 19 | 24 | 17 | 7 | 22 | 21 |
| Patrick Le Rolland | Cramique | France | 332-262 | 29 | 7 | 20 | 29 | 28 | 22 | 23 | 22 |
| Jennie Loriston-Clarke | Kadett | Great Britain | 299-270 | 26 | 15 | 26 | 22 | 24 | 11 | 24 | 22 |
| Silvio M. de Rezende | Othelo | Brazil | 304-262 | 29 | 24 | 22 | 23 | 25 | 7 | 25 | 26 |
| Cynthia Neal | Bonne Année | Canada | 307-267 | 27 | 27 | 29 | 20 | 16 | 13 | 26 | 25 |
| Friederica Benedictus | Turista | Netherlands | 301-266 | 22 | 32 | 28 | 26 | 21 | 11 | 27 | 27 |
| John Swaab | Maharadscha | Netherlands | 300-260 | 31 | 28 | 24 | 25 | 27 | 7 | 28 | 29 |
| Maria Äschbacher | Charlamp | Switzerland | 301-247 | 20 | 26 | 23 | 32 | 29 | 12 | 29 | 28 |
| Lorraine Stubbs | Venezuela | Canada | 296-263 | 28 | 30 | 27 | 28 | 30 | 3 | 30 | 31 |
| Lois Stephens | Fasching | U.S.A. | 278-254 | 23 | 25 | 30 | 31 | 32 | 9 | 31 | 30 |
| Kikuko Inoue | Don Carlos | Japan | 270-252 | 32 | 33 | 32 | 30 | 31 | 3 | 32 | 32 |
| Margret D. Lawrence | San Fernando | Great Britain | 267-239 | 33 | 31 | 33 | 33 | 33 | 2 | 33 | 33 |

ter that he does not allow himself to be influenced in any way in his judging but puts his entire knowledge and understanding into the cause. Chauvinism, from which we have unfortunately not yet freed ourselves, is just as objectionable as lack of knowledge or the inability to express an opinion of one's own. A judge of that kind should have no place in small national horse shows and certainly none at an event such as the Olympic Games.

Not only the experts but also other attentive observers were struck by the large differences in the evaluations of the dressage riders in Munich. Part of the press, as an excuse, pointed out that the judges placed on the short side of the dressage arena had a different field of vision than those seated on the long sides. Fundamentally, this statement is correct. The judge seated at the front of the arena may see many things better than the judge seated at the side. On the other hand, the judges placed on the sides have a better view than the rest of the judges of many faults that may occur during the frequent turns from one long side of the arena to the other required in this test. However, the comparison of results I have charted clearly shows that the serious differences in place marks were to be found among the three judges placed on the short sides of the arena. Here the difference between the highest and the lowest place marks was of:

0 to 4 places with 13 riders
5 places with 1 rider
6 places with 4 riders
7 places with 3 riders
8 places with 2 riders
9 places with 3 riders
10 places with 2 riders

and with one rider respectively 11, 12, 13, 14, and 22 places.

With the two judges seated at the long sides of the arena, the difference in the place marks was of:

> 0 to 4 places with 22 riders
> 5 places with   3 riders
> 6 places with   1 rider
> 7 places with   4 riders

and with 1 rider respectively, 8, 11, and 12 places.

Indeed as already remarked, it is sometimes very difficult for a judge to evaluate with justice if the performances of the riders are of a low standard. It is even more difficult to place the riders correctly if there are thirty or more on an equal level. The conscientious judge would admit that it is practically impossible to be absolutely just in his evaluation even with the utmost impartiality when he sees so large a number of riders in only one test. He should therefore welcome the opportunity to see the riders a second time, as is the case now in the ride-off.

When studying the names of the judges who composed the juries of the Grand Prix de Dressage at the Olympic Games in the past decades it is with surprise and consternation that one notes that quite a few of them were never dressage riders and cannot boast of any achievements in this sphere, such as winning trophies or being outstanding as teachers. When there is a music contest of any international importance nowadays, nobody totally unknown in this field would be called into the jury. Therefore, it is doubly incomprehensible that dressage judges often come from countries that have never delegated any riders to compete or who have not participated for several decades. How could such judges give a clear concept for the riders if they themselves have never demonstrated in practice the correctness of their ideas?

At the Olympic Games, as the greatest athletic event, supreme performances should be expected from all participants. Therefore once more: the best riders of the world deserve the best judges of the world.

And as with previous Olympic contests, the dressage tests in the beautiful Nymphenburger Park produced a scandal, which, however, this time did not spring from chauvinism as in Stockholm in 1956. It was inconceivable from the outset that a rider with a lame horse was allowed to ride the test through to the end and even more so that he was placed twenty-ninth by two judges, twenty-eighth by the third, and twentieth by his compatriot. It is downright shocking, however, that one of the judges awarded him seventh place in a field of thirty-three riders. Any further comment is superfluous and it is to be hoped that the FEI investigated the matter.

The spectators, very well behaved otherwise, made their decision there and then and gave vent to their opinion by booing loudly.

# 8

# Criteria of
# Classical Riding

During a dressage test the judge is expected to make quick decisions. His gifts of observation and discernment must be based on a solid equestrian knowledge, gained not only in the saddle but also at the judge's stand. The judge-to-be must first of all learn what to look for, how to see and to distinguish.

Just as the great riding master Max Ritter von Weyrother, one of the most famous head riders of the Spanish Riding School in Vienna, required at the beginning of training that the young horse learn to move correctly, I want to begin by discussing the three basic paces of the horse.

At the walk the horse advances in a diagonal sequence of steps putting one foot after the other forward so that four distinct hoof beats may be seen and heard. It is a bad fault in this pace if the horse moves both the foreleg and hind leg of the same side simultaneously. This is called a pace or amble, an unnatural motion which the expert may clearly see in the rider's rocking seat. To pace at the walk is a grave offence against the concept of the purity of the gaits. In the Grand Prix de Dressage as well as in any other test it must be severely penalized in all exercises at the walk and, of course, in the general remarks at the end, for it impairs the value of the entire performance. Moreover, this defective walk reveals incorrect training of the horse which becomes visible also in the other exercises.

At the walk the sequence of steps should remain unchanged in the various tempi—medium, collected, and extended walk. What should change are the length and elevation of the stride. Consequently, just as with faulty tempo in the other paces, so with the walk there should be severe penalty points for a horse that does not maintain an even rhythm, that takes some longer and some shorter strides, becomes hasty and trips. At the walk, just as in the other paces, the regularity of the movement is the supreme requirement. The horse must not move along by dragging his feet but take solemn strides. At the extended walk he should cover so much ground to the front that his hind legs overreach the hoof prints of his forefeet. Unfortunately, the evaluation of dressage tests often neglects these requirements, for it happens even in the most advanced classes that horses with the above-mentioned faults, sometimes even with a clear amble, end up among the top scorers.

At the trot the diagonal pairs of legs are lifted off the ground simultaneously and are put down again simultaneously. In between the horse remains off the ground with all four feet for a moment. This is called the moment of suspension. At the trot greater demands are made upon the balance of not only the horse but also the rider. The entire weight of horse and rider alternately rests on one diagonal pair of legs before and after the moment of suspension. The sequence of steps remains the same at the medium, collected, and extended trot. The difference is in the length of the stride and the duration of the moment of suspension. The latter is shortest at the collected and longest at the extended tempo. The rhythmic movement of the diagonal pairs of legs must remain the same at all tempi; it is the length of stride that changes. Shortening the stride for the collected tempo while maintaining the rhythm naturally causes the legs to be lifted higher. The sequence of steps must never become slower, as is so often seen in dressage tests and should be scored accordingly. Close observation of these and other details, such as the horse's hind legs stepping straight under his body or the simultaneous footfall of the diagonal pair of legs, enables the judge to form a comprehensive verdict.

The canter consists of a series of bounds. At the various tempi—medium, collected, and extended—it must be performed at an even rhythm of three beats. This is possible only if the horse has sufficient impulsion and suppleness. The four-beat canter often seen is an impure pace which strikes the non-expert who has a feeling for harmony as a particularly ugly hobbling movement. The judge must immediately detect and penalize it as a severe fault, just as he will give negative marks to the canter on the wrong lead or the disunited canter. Let's never forget the basic requirement: the purity of the paces.

In the flying change at the canter on the center line or when changing over the diagonal of the arena, the judge can observe whether the horse takes a full stride to the front with his hind legs, whether he remains straight or throws his weight to the side and becomes crooked. Such faults must not be overlooked, for they point to a deficiency in the basic concept of training. Interspersing simple changes of canter when practising the flying changes of lead is highly recommended. It prevents the horse from anticipating the rider's aids and makes him wait for them. A test with similar alternations of exercises allows the judge to draw conclusions about the degree of the rider's leading role in the presentation of his horse. Scoring the flying change at the medium canter is another means to help the judge place the competitors in the correct sequence, especially with a large number of participants. The judge may draw conclusions as to the impulsion, correctness, and liveliness of the movement, the regularity and purity of the paces, the precision with which the exercises are performed and which may be taken as proof of the horse's obedience from the following exercises: the performance of serpentines through the whole arena in four to six loops at the canter with a simple or flying change of lead when changing rein or without a change of canter presenting one loop at the true and the following loop at the counter canter; or the serpentine at the counter canter with a change of lead at every change of rein—that is, simple or flying change of lead from one counter canter to the next. Close observation of all those details is the basis of just evaluation.

What faults should the judge particularly watch out for? Which of the faults is more aggravating? There is so much talk about impulsion, about freedom and lightness. How and in which exercises do these fundamental requirements of a dressage horse manifest themselves? When scoring, the judge is obliged to take these fundamentals into consideration no matter whether the rider is competing in a beginner's class or in one of the Fifth Level. Basically, it is far more important to prevent the young rider or the young horse at the beginning of their career from deviating from the correct way of training and not to allow a false concept to take root.

The object of the collaboration of horse and rider must be to maintain the horse's natural paces and impulsion and by systematic training to develop them to the highest degree of perfection. When faults occur, the dressage judge must be fully aware of whether it is a basic deficiency or some obvious but unimportant error. He must express his opinion accordingly in his scores and the general remarks.

It is one of the fundamental requirements of any good riding horse that he move straight and forward. In other words, his hind legs should step into the direction of his forefeet or into their hoof prints. It is interesting to note that the ancient masters were caused no headaches when striving for this principle which corresponds to the natural movement of the horse when at liberty. Once they have become accustomed to the rider's weight and the rhythm of the movement, most horses have little difficulty with this problem when ridden on long straight lines cross country and even on roads. It is work in an arena, that is, in restricted space with turns following each other in rapid succession, that crookedness became a problem which has entailed much discussion and many attempts to straighten the horse.

The French riding master Pluvinel (1626) in his book *Le Manège Royal* tried to explain this crookedness, which he believed he detected particularly on the right side, by supposing it to be due to the position of the foal in the mare's womb. His compatriot Guérinière (1733), in order to combat crookedness, invented shoulder-in and practised it especially on that side. As early as 1588, Löhneysen stated that because of the crookedness at the canter on the right lead the horse should be worked on that rein more often than on the other.

Louis Seeger was a pupil of the riding master Max Ritter von Weyrother, mentioned previously, to whose influence we owe the chapter about "Equestrian Training" in the rules of training for the Austro-Hungarian cavalry. Seeger in his book *System of the Art of Riding*, published in 1844, opposed the theory that the horse had an increased tendency to be crooked to the right. He believed the cause of crookedness to be the fact that the horse's body is narrower through the shoulders than through the hips. The practical experience during the training of my chargers and dressage horses has caused me to adopt his opinion. If the shoulder of the horse and his hind quarters remain at an equal distance from the wall of the arena, the inside hind foot cannot step into the direction of the hoof print of the foreleg of the same side but must step to the side of it. Consequently, the horse becomes crooked. In my book *The Complete Training of Horse and Rider* I have explained how to correct this fault, which may seriously impair any further training. Steinbrecht, who was strongly influenced by the Spanish Riding School of Vienna, has coined the phrase that embraces the principles of equestrian training and that every rider should choose for his leitmotif: "Straighten your horse and ride him forward." From my own practical experience I should like to express this excellent advice in the following recommendation: "If you ride your horse forward with sufficient impulsion he will remain straight!"

Guided by this principle, I never had any difficulty riding those horses straight forward that I trained from the beginning. I became acquainted with crookedness when I first rode the horses of my pupils. At the same time I discovered how infinitely more difficult it is to straighten a horse that has acquired the habit of placing the hind quarters into the arena, especially at the canter. Moreover, I found out that a horse's crookedness does not occur on his right side only but individually depends on his greater suppleness on one side and stiffness on the other.

In the interest of further training a rider should be expected to present a horse going straight and forward even in a beginner's class. For the same reason the judge should always mark severely a horse that is crooked, for his training does not meet with the most elementary requirements. Severity on this subject benefits not only the young rider but also dressage riding in general.

Impulsion and correct contact, which are required in any dressage test, depend upon the straightness of the horse. Consequently, any uneven or unilateral contact with the bit or a lack of forward urge in the movement may be caused by crookedness. They become noticeable in the lack of suppleness and lightness, with the horse opposing the action of the rein and often taking uneven steps. These elementary requirements of a dressage horse should be complied with in the beginner's classes before any further demands are made. Here the judge will fulfill his task only if he penalizes such faults by marking insufficient or even less.

The expert eye of the judge will have proof of the horse's straightness if the hind legs step into the hoof prints of the forelegs or into their direction. This is best seen from the side. Looking from the front or from the rear the judge watches for the hind quarters to be swung away from the wall of the arena. In this case the hind legs step to the side of the hoof prints of the forefeet. However, one might be misled when looking after a horse ridden away from the judge. A horse with broad hind quarters may convey the impression that he is crooked. It is to the horse's feet that the judge must direct his attention. A horse should be observed in the same way when performing a circle or volte. Even on a curved line the horse is expected to move straight, that is, his hind legs following the hoof prints of the forelegs. At the same time the judge may note whether the circle or volte is truly round. Only a horse going straight can perform a correct circle.

In a double volte at the canter the rhythm of the collected canter should be the same as when on a straight line or at the counter canter. Both voltes must be identical, supplementing each other, two circles each of six steps' diameter, and absolutely round. The hind legs must jump straight into the direction of the hoof prints of the forelegs. This exercise is to be ridden in the same manner at the collected trot. The horse must maintain the same rhythm as when on a straight line. It is interesting to note that this relatively simple exercise gives trouble to horse and rider even in the most advanced classes. To the judge it points infallibly to deficiencies in basic training. In half voltes and turns at the collected trot or canter the judge should watch for the horse to perform the exercise on a single track. Especially when returning to the wall he should move on an oblique line but on a single track. The horse must not become crooked or try to push back to the wall in a sort of half pass.

Many horses have a tendency, especially at the canter, to swing the hind quarters into the arena before passing through a corner or making a turn. This occurs also before a half or full pirouette. Besides crookedness this fault reveals the horse's anticipation of the rider's aids, which counts among the deficiencies in basic training.

While the horse passes through a corner of the arena, the judge watches to see whether the horse throws his weight on his inside shoulder. For in this case he is not straight and his hind feet do not follow his forelegs. At the same time the corner cannot be performed in the prescribed way, that is, on a radius of six steps. A rider who passes correctly through a corner even if performing a larger arc is to be awarded higher scores than one who respects the prescribed measures but loses rhythm and balance. This is to be especially remembered in beginners' classes.

When changing over the diagonal through the whole arena at the trot as well as at the canter it is important that the horse perform a straight line from one determined mark to the other. He must not sway along this line or lose the direction by pushing to one side. Such deficiencies are much graver than is generally assumed. They may not be explained by inattentiveness of the rider but are due to faulty contact with the bit, lack of impulsion and straightness, or tenseness of the horse. At the canter there is the additional need to observe whether the horse moves at a regular rhythm of three beats and maintains it in the proper sequence of the bounds. Closely related to straightening the horse is the contact with the bit which alone allows the correct physical training of the horse. The traditional expression "contact" means that it is the horse that should seek the contact with the rider's hand. It should not be reversed, the rider trying to force the horse into a determined position of his head by means of the rein aids. This principle should be a guideline for every rider and trainer. And the judge should take it as a

criterion, for by his severe verdict he should counteract
the frequent endeavour of some riders to impose a position of head and neck to the horse by means of lever-like
rein aids and torturous bits. At all periods of time there
have been brutal riding masters who never grasped the
essence of the art of riding, which is the fusion of the endeavours of two creatures into one. Their methods remained a warning, an example which deterred riders
from practising dressage, as happened in the country of
the Duke of Newcastle, where dressage riding was ob-
jected to until the beginning of our century.

The correct contact with the bit may be best perceived
when both reins are lightly applied and the horse follows
the most discreet action of the rein to increase the lateral
position, to execute a turn, or to perform other exercises,
especially voltes, serpentines, half voltes, and changes of
direction. Much information may be gained from observing the rider's hands. A rider who in these exercises sepa-
rates his hands certainly does not turn his horse by a delicate action of the rein. From the steady position of the
rider's hands, on the contrary, the judge may conclude
the horse's steady contact with the bit.

Mutual understanding, too, is proved by the steady
contact with the bit, the horse concentrating on his rider
and trusting willingly to his guidance with unreserved
confidence. The horse's peaceful expression, his ears
turned attentively toward the rider, his mouth closed,
quiet, and moist with foam, are all symptoms of correct
contact with the bit. In contrast, the horse constantly
playing with his lips, his mouth dry and often open, his
tongue pulled up or placed over the bit, his restless ears
and changing degree of contact point unmistakably to un-

satisfactory contact with the bit, which the judge must take into account in his scores.

Uneven contact with the bit results in stiffness of the horse on one side and exaggerated position to the other. In most cases the horse maintains this exaggerated position to one side on both reins, which may best be observed from the front. Uneven contact becomes most noticeable in the performance of lines and figures. Turns, voltes, or serpentines will be executed in a different way on the different reins. Consequently, it must not be taken for carelessness on the part of the rider if, for instance, a volte on the right rein is performed larger or smaller than on the left rein. It is, on the contrary, to be marked as a grave fault, for it proves deficient contact with the bit.

Any resistance, even the slightest, such as throwing the head up or tilting it in the transitions into lower paces or to a halt, is proof of non-consolidated contact with the bit as well as lack of lightness and suppleness.

On the other hand, the judge should beware of mere fault-seeking. He should mark the positive moments of a performance just as conscientiously as he would the deficiencies. For instance, any absolute immobility at the halt with correct position of head and neck as well as the immediate departure from the standstill into the desired pace without any change of position should be scored highly as proof of faultless contact with the bit and the correct use of the aids on the part of the rider.

Lack of lightness, which does not allow the action of the reins to pass through the body of the horse and influence his hind legs, becomes most obvious in the rein-back. Here is a deficiency which the judge must not overlook, for it is of great influence on the scoring in any class and even more so in a beginners' class. There is ample opportunity in this exercise for the judge to observe the regularity of the sequence of the horse's steps. He should simultaneously lift the diagonal pair of legs—for instance, right fore and left hind foot—off the ground and put them back and down at the same time and at the same rhythm, continuing with the other pair of legs in the same manner. In case the feet do not touch the ground at the same moment the movement must be severely marked down as an impure pace. For the purity of the paces, once again, is the governing law of classical horsemanship.

Resistance against the action of the rein not only points to lack of lightness but also proves incorrect contact with the bit, which is always present if the rider tries to force the position of the horse's head by means of the reins alone, that is, when he does not allow the horse to seek the contact with the bit.

Another means of ascertaining the lightness of the horse to the action of the rein is offered by the transitions from movement into the halt or from one pace into another as well in the changes of tempo within the same pace. These exercises may be less striking to the non-expert, but the judge should follow their performance very attentively. Provided these transitions come about without the slightest difference in the contact with the bit, they prove exemplary lightness and suppleness which is to be rewarded with bonus points.

The change of tempo between medium and extended trot and vice versa must be so clearly defined that the point at which the change of speed is performed should be exactly visible.

The transition from the collected canter into the medium trot should be executed with suppleness and in a distinct forward movement. From the impulsion at the trot the judge may expect a lively collected canter. Generally speaking, true impulsion may best be seen in collection. It is not the wind singing in the rider's ears that proves the impulsion of a movement. It is the powerful and elevated steps with which the horse moves in the collected paces. The moment of suspension must be distinctly visible. At the extended trot the judge should not be fooled by the hectically strutting forelegs but watch for the gain of ground to the front and note whether and how far the hind legs step under the body of the horse. From the relation of the movement of forehand and hind quarters comes the true gain of ground. Goose-stepping front legs, in most cases are accompanied by irregular steps of the hind legs which cannot follow in the same rhythm. Again this fault is to be severely penalized as an offence against the required purity of the paces.

I want to underline once more that the phenomena enumerated here are relevant to the basic training which must be required from any dressage horse regardless of the class or the level of advancement. Rider and teacher should be well aware of this fact. In the same measure it should guide the judge in his observation and scoring. It must be understood by all three of them that this is the only basis on which the training of a dressage horse may develop to the highest degrees.

# In Memoriam
# Alois Podhajsky

Alois Podhajsky passed away on May 23, 1973. The death of this great rider and teacher put an end to the relation between author and publisher which had proved fruitful in a rare manner and which had grown into friendship. Podhajsky's most important work, *The Complete Training of Horse and Rider in the Principles of Classical Horsemanship*, has influenced the development of riding in all countries as the reference book indispensable to rider and teacher alike. In this book Podhajsky has laid down and enlarged the training regulations of the Spanish Riding School which had never before appeared in print but had been handed down by word of mouth. There is nothing in this book that Podhajsky had not proved and approved by his own experience.

Ann Tizia Leitich, a well-known Austrian author, wrote about Colonel Podhajsky: "Very slim and tall, he seems to be one with his stallion. His lean face expresses stone-like calmness, intense concentration and an almost religious dedication to the cause. Later, in his office and in the elegant salons of the Spanish Riding School he meets us with democratic unaffectedness like the personification of the spirit that through centuries has been the very essence of the noble art of riding. . . ."

In 1960 I was able to publish Podhajsky's first book, *Ein Leben für die Lipizzaner*, his autobiography, which in English is known under the title *My Dancing White Horses*. His last work, on the problems of fair judging, deals with a subject that had fascinated him all his life. To him justice is a goal. Maybe it is connected with another important element in riding, balance. At first it is an outward balance which gradually develops into inner harmony. This is the rider's reward; it contains educational values and the moral obligation to be fair and just with your horse. "He should be," says Podhajsky, "your friend."

Podhajsky as an author is synonymous with clarity in argumentation, respect for tradition, severe criticism of any shortcomings, evaluation of the demands made upon the horse by criteria based upon the observation of the horse at liberty. In addition, there is Podhajsky's critical but clear-sighted attitude towards himself and towards others. When justice was at stake he was free from any traditional constraint. If necessary he defended his opinion with vehemence. Having approved of a cause, he fought for it.

In Podhajsky's books the reader is struck by his use of the language. It is the author's endeavour to see the art of riding understood as a constant flow, alternating, as in life, expectation and fulfillment, high tide and low tide, effort and relaxation. Podhajsky's favourite words are: evenness, understanding, simplicity, music, rhythm, art. And on the other hand: self-control, self-knowledge, striving, correctness, poise, subordination, regularity, achievement.

In every one of these words and in the severe ones in particular, there is a demand. First of all, a demand made upon oneself, and then only upon others. This was Podhajsky's program. In its striving for educational values it was not modern in the superficial sense of the word. In the tempest of time Podhajsky was a keeper and a guardian. He was the man who saved the Spanish Riding School of Vienna. He was a great teacher. He was the preserver of the classical art of riding. These are his historical merits.

Podhajsky was a seeker; he was a humble and grateful man. He was a friend.

When his first wife had passed away he found a second companion, Eva Podhajsky, who became his support and assistant. She translated several of his books into English. She helped him to cope with a full day's work to which, in these last years, was again added the joy of working with horses. He was active until a week before his death. His last thoughts were for this book, about to be concluded.

In the name of his friends in all the world, of the readers of his books, I want to say thank you to Alois Podhajsky. Our gratitude goes to the author of these books which teach the difficult, the gentle art of riding. To Alois Podhajsky.

Berthold Spangenberg

*Munich, 1973*

# Index

American Horse Shows
Association (AHSA), 2
Angular voltes, 39
Äschbacher, Maria, 115–16,
161
Assyrians (ancient), 15–16

Benedictus, Friederica, 110,
125–26, 161
Bernhard, Prince of the
Netherlands, 89
Biel, Baron G., 20
Blixen-Finecke, Lieutenant von,
72
Boldt, 93
Boltenstern, Captain, 72, 82
Bonde, Captain Count, 72
Breuil, General de, 110
Brockmüller, Gerhard, 161

Chamberlain, Major, 75
Chammartin, 93
Classical riding, criteria of,
165–77; the canter, 167;
changing over diagonal of
arena, 167–68, 173; contact
with the bit, 173–76; faults
to watch for, 168–69;
impulsion of a movement,
171, 176–77; straightness
of the horse, 169–73; at the
trot, 166–67; at the walk,
165–67. *See also* Riding
Collected canter, 43–44, 47, 48;

counter changes at, 50;
double serpentine at, 44; half
pass at, 49–50
Collected trot: half pass at,
49–50; half pirouette at,
47–48
Collective Marks, 93, 95–96,
98; introduction of (at Rome
Olympics, 1960), 90–91
Combined judging method,
59–61; advantages and
disadvantages of, 63–64;
preliminary test in, 60–61
*Complete Training of Horse
and Rider in the Principles of
Classical Horsemanship*
(Podhajsky), 6, 25, 170,
178
Concours de Dressage (1937),
81
Concours de Dressage
International Officiel
(DCIO), 77
*Concours hippique*, 55
Concours Hippique in
Frankfurt (1910), 62
Concours Hippique in Turin
(1902), 62
Coubertin, Pierre de, 70–71
Counter canter, 46

Diem, Carl, 71
Doorne, Annie van, 110,
126–27, 161

Double bridle, 35–36, 40, 45
Double voltes, 46
Dressage competitions:
  requirements for, 3; scoring
  of, 3–4
Dressage tests, requirements of,
  26–54; classification of, 26;
  of FEI, 27, 47–48, 54; Fifth
  Level, 25, 26, 27, 44, 48–54,
  168; First Level, 26, 29–35,
  40, 41, 45; Fourth Level, 26,
  34, 44, 45–47; international
  level, 44–45, 47–48, 54;
  judging of, 1, 20–25, 28–29;
  meaning of, 55; most
  important demand for,
  22–23; paces and steps,
  27–28; Second Level, 26,
  35–40, 41, 47, 54; Third
  Level, 26, 35, 40–44, 45, 47,
  54
Dür, Hermann, 113–14, 161

Ein Leben für die Lipizzaner
  (Podhajsky), 179

Fédération Equestre
  Internationale (FEI), 2, 3,
  18, 60, 61, 66, 70, 75, 77,
  89, 96, 111, 164; dressage
  tests of, 27, 47–48, 54;
  founded, 73; method of
  judging, 63
Fifth Level (test), 25, 26, 27,
  44, 48–54, 168; balance, 51;
  counter changes at collected
  canter, 50; flying changes of
  lead, 52–53; half pass at
  collected trot and canter,
  49–50; judging, 58, 61, 62;
  piaffe and passage, 53–54;
  pirouettes, 52; rein-back, 51;
  short half passes (zigzags),
  50–51; shoulder-in on center
  line, 49; at the walk, 48–49;
  walk and canter, 51–52
Filatow, 90, 93
First Level (test), 26, 29–35,
  40, 41, 45; correct contact

with the bit, 33; halt, 32;
  importance of, 29–30;
  judging, 60, 62; jump, 34;
  paces, walk, trot, and canter,
  30–32; rein-back, 32–33;
  rider's seat and attitude,
  33–34; tempo, 31
Fischer, 90
Fourth Level (test), 26, 34, 44,
  45–47; correctness of halt,
  47; extended walk, 45;
  haunches-in, or travers,
  haunches-out, or renvers, 46;
  judging, 58, 61, 62; jump,
  47; lateral exercises, 46–47;
  trot and canter, 45, 46; use
  of reins, 46

Gerhard, Major, 76
Giving the reins, 37–38
Grand Prix de Dressage. See
  Olympic Games
Grand Prix with a ride-off
  (test), 27
Guérinière, 17, 19, 27–28,
  169

Hakansson, Ulla, 110, 111,
  122–23, 146–47, 160
Half voltes, 39, 47
Hansen, Christilot, 136–37,
  147–48, 160
Hartel, Lis, 85, 87
Haute Ecole (High School),
  18, 21, 25, 91, 155, 156
Herrera, 110
Heydebreck, 17
Hittites (ancient), 15
Höbert, General, 34

Ingemann, Charlotte, 140–41,
  161
Inoue, Kikuko, 143–44, 161
Intermediate Test, 27
International Equestrian
  Federation. See Fédération
  Equestre Internationale
  (FEI)

*International Equitation at the
   Olympic Games of 1936*
   (Rau), 62
International Olympic
   Committee, 89

Johnstone, Lorna, 109–10,
   130–31, 153–54, 160
Joussaume, Colonel, 82, 85
Judges, duties of, 9–14
Judging, 1, 9–14, 20–25,
   28–29; in Austria, 55, 57–58,
   61–62; combined method of,
   59–61, 63–64; demand for
   open judging, 64–65; FEI
   method of, 63; guidelines,
   20–25; and misjudgement,
   56–57; at the Olympic
   Games (1912–1968),
   70–96; preliminary test,
   57–58, 60, 61, 62; separate
   method of, 61–63, 66;
   systems of, 55–69

Kalita, Iwan, 117–18, 149, 160
Kisimov, Ivan, 94, 116–17,
   144–45, 160
Klimke, 94
Köhler, Horst, 131–32, 161
Kür, 27; exercises performed in,
   54

Langen, Baron von, 74
Lawrence, Margret D.,
   129–30, 161
Leitich, Ann Tizia, 178
Le Rolland, Patrick, 110, 142,
   161
Lesage, Captain, 74, 75
Linder, General, 73
Linsenhoff, Liselott, 87, 97,
   110, 111, 119–20,
   145–46, 160
Lipizzaner Stud Farm, 73
Löhneysen, 169–70
Loriston-Clarke, Jennie,
   128–29, 161
Lundblad, Captain, 73

*Manège Royal, Le* (Pluvinel),
   169
Marion, Major, 74, 75
Master, Edith, 133–34, 161
Mikkelsen, Aksel, 139–40,
   148, 160
Moser, Captain, 82
Müller, Wolfgang, 132–33,
   161

Neal, Cynthia, 138–39, 161
Neckermann, Josef, 90, 94, 98,
   110, 111, 121–22, 152, 160
Nishi, Lieutenant, 75
*Noble Horse, The* (Biel), 20
Nyblaeus, Colonel, 110

Oeynhausen, 17
Olsen, 74
Olympic Games (776 B.C. to
   A.D. 393), 71
Olympic Games (1896), 71
Olympic Games (1900), 71
Olympic Games (1908), 71
Olympic Games (1912), 71,
   72–73
Olympic Games (1920), 73
Olympic Games (1924), 73
Olympic Games (1928), 74
Olympic Games (1932), 74–76
Olympic Games (1936), 64,
   76–81, 86, 89; method of
   marking, 79–80; number of
   jury members, 79;
   participating nations, 76–77;
   tests required at, 77–79
Olympic Games (1948),
   82–84, 86, 87
Olympic Games (1952),
   84–88, 157
Olympic Games (1956),
   87–90, 155, 164
Olympic Games (1960),
   90–92, 157; introduction of
   Collective Marks at, 90–91,
   94; participating nations, 90
Olympic Games (1964),
   92–94, 157

Olympic Games (1968), 93,
94–96, 157
Olympic Games (1972), 64,
65, 66, 97–164; comparison
of results of principal test,
160–61; criticism of judges
and judging, 158–64; Grand
Prix de Dressage (Principal
Test), 99–102; jury
members, 110–11;
participating nations, 97;
Podhajsky's observations of,
111–13; Ride-Off (test),
103–5; ride-off for individual
medalists, 144–54; riders
(principal test), 113–44;
Three-Day Event, 98
Open judging, 158; demand
for, 64–65
Oval voltes, 39

Patton, General George S., Jr.,
72–73
Petersen, Ulla, 161
Petuschkowa, Elena, 97,
118–19, 141–42, 151–52,
160
Piaffe, 21, 24, 52, 78, 85–86,
91, 155; balance and
performance of, 25; at the
Fifth Level, 53–54
Pirouettes, 47–48, 52, 78, 91,
107–8
Pluvinel, 17, 169
Podhajsky, Alois, 178–80
Pollay, Colonel, 76, 110
Pongracz, General von, 62,
64–65
Pot, Mr., 110
Prix St. George (test), 27

Rau, Gustave, 62
Rein-back, 32–33, 37–38, 44,
51
Rezende, Silvio M. de, 142–43,
161
Riding, 15–25; in ancient
times, 15–16, 17; classical
concept of, 17–18; demands

of, 20–25; Germanic or
Romanic styles of, 18–19,
42, 87; importance of
balance, 7; physical and
mental requirements for, 5–8;
principles of, 12–13,
17–18. See also Classical
riding; Judging; names of
riders
Riding Teacher, The
(Podhajsky), 6, 7
Rosen, Count Clarence von,
71–72, 73, 110, 111
Rosen, Maud von, 124–25,
152–53, 160

St. Cyr, Major, 85, 87
Sandström, Lieutenant, 73
Schlüter, Karin, 110, 111,
120–21, 149–50, 160
Second Level (test), 26,
35–40, 41, 47, 54; canter,
37, 38–40; change of lead,
38; judging, 58, 60, 62;
jump, 40; rein-back, 37–38;
rider's position, 40; snaffle
and double bridle, 35–36;
tempo, 37; turn on the
haunches, 40; voltes, 39;
walk and trot, 36–37
Seeger, Louis, 170
Separate judging method,
61–63, 66; advantages and
disadvantages of, 63–64; in
Austria, 62–63
Serpentines, riding, 34, 46,
175; double, at the collected
canter, 44; of four loops,
42–43
Snaffle, 35
Socrates, 16
Spanish Riding School of
Vienna, 20, 72–73, 170,
179, 180
Sportsmanship, lack of, 28–29
Steinbrecht, 17
Stensbeck, 17
Stephens, Lois, 135–36, 161

Stubbs, Lorraine, 137–38, 161
Stückelberger, Christine, 114–15, 161
Swaab, John, 110, 111, 127–28, 161
Swaab, Ninna, 123–24, 150–51, 160
*System of The Art of Riding* (Seeger), 170

Third Level (test), 26, 35, 40–44, 45, 47, 54; at the collected canter, 43–44; haunches at the walk, 42; judging, 58, 60, 62; jump, 44; lateral exercise at, 41–42; rein-back, 44; serpentines, 42–43; tempo, 43; walk and canter, 43, 44

Tuttle, Captain, 75

Voltes, performance of, 24, 32, 39, 46, 47, 50, 172, 175

Weyrother, Max Ritter von, 17, 20, 165, 170
Winnett, John, 134–35, 161
World Exposition at Paris (1900), 71
*World History of Sport and Physical Exercise* (Diem), 71
World War I, 71
World War II, 56, 71, 82

Xenophon, 16, 19

Yielding to the leg, 34

Zigzags, 50–51
*Zügel aus der Hand kauen,* 38